*Cycling i*

C000253851

# CYCLING IS MY LIFE

## Tommy Simpson

YELLOW JERSEY PRESS
LONDON

First published by Stanley Paul & Co Ltd in 1966

Published by Yellow Jersey Press 2009

4 6 8 10 9 7 5 3

Published in Great Britain in 2009 by
Yellow Jersey Press
Random House, 20 Vauxhall Bridge Road,
London SW1V 2SA

www.rbooks.co.uk

Addresses for companies within The Random House Group Limited
can be found at: www.randomhouse.co.uk/offices.htm

The Random House Group Limited Reg. No. 954009

A CIP catalogue record for this book
is available from the British Library

ISBN 9780224083089

Penguin Random House is committed to a sustainable future for
our business, our readers and our planet. This book is made from
Forest Stewardship Council® certified paper.

Printed and bound in Great Britain by Clays Ltd, St Ives plc

# Contents

Off the bike I am naturally lazy and would never have written this without the advice and constant prodding of David Saunders. To him my grateful thanks.

# Introduction by David Millar

Tommy Simpson is a name that holds a certain resonance in the world of cycling. For in the one hundred years the modern sport of road racing has existed, Simpson stands head and shoulders above his compatriots.

Bicycle road racing was killed in its infancy in Great Britain – those that governed banished competitive cycling from the roads to remove the nuisance they perceived it to be – and so bike racing became a cult underground movement practised in different forms by many but seen by few. Meanwhile, across the Channel, cycling was blossoming. It rapidly became the people's sport. The masses respected and cheered their great riders but they rarely envied them: they realised the sheer suffering entailed in fulfilling the extraordinary demands race promoters put upon these 'kings of the road' in the name of spectacle and story-telling.

The British had dominated cycling at the end of the nineteenth century – they were world leaders both in manufacturing and as competitors – but with time this has become but a distant forgotten memory. The Tour de France would exist for over sixty years before a British rider was to wear the coveted yellow jersey, and of the seven most prestigious one-day races held each season, the Classics, still only four have been won by a Brit. In 2008 Sir Chris Hoy became the second cyclist to win BBC Sports Personality of the year; the first – the man who had become the first Briton to wear the yellow jersey and the only Briton to win four Classics – was Tommy Simpson. It would be another thirty years before a Briton wore the yellow jersey again; another forty before a Briton would win even one Classic. These were Tommy's feats, what we in cycling call his '*palmarès*'.

Tommy Simpson was certainly not the first British cyclist to cross the Channel and enter the other world known as the Continent. There had been other riders before him who inspired his initial move to Brittany. But he was the first to charm all Europe not only with his ability to race but with his personality and panache. Far removed from his roots in post-war Yorkshire, he became a star in France, one of the '*Grands*' in the sport of professional road racing. And these are the reasons why the name 'Tommy Simpson' still resonates with pride, respect and fondness. But Tommy's *palmarès* are not his only legacy.

I too am a professional road racer. I have been since I was nineteen years old. At thirty-two I am now older than Tommy was when he died. He was in his thirtieth year when he collapsed one kilometre from the summit of Mont Ventoux during the 1967 Tour de France. There is a memorial to him on that spot, and every time I pass it I am in the habit of doffing what in my younger years was a cloth cap, but has since become a helmet, to his memory. It is a memory I hold closer than most, because he is a person I can relate to more than most. Tommy Simpson and I share many traits and have followed similar paths. I, like him, immersed myself completely in a world that was very foreign to me in the pursuit of a dream. As with Tommy, that dream became life-consuming; as with Tommy, it ended up with my doping. But I have survived where Tommy didn't.

Mont Ventoux, the Windy Mountain, the Giant of Provence. It's not a nice place to die, and it wasn't a nice way to die, and we have no right to forget that. Tommy's memory should live on, through his *palmarès* and the memories of his friends, family, fans and the books and articles written about him. But, above all, his memory should live on through the mistakes he made and the price he paid. He died from doping at a time when there was no doping control. His death was a wake-up call that years later we are only starting to hear. This is Tommy Simpson's legacy.

Forty years to the day after Tommy's death, 13 July 2007, I was riding the sixth stage of the ninety-fourth Tour de France. There was not even a mention of Tommy's legacy. That was the day I realised just how far the sport had to go before it could rectify all the wrongs it had allowed. Even while professional cycling claimed to be doing everything within its power to change the hardened doping culture that existed, I knew that something was desperately wrong. We were teetering on the edge of an abyss. It was as if Tommy Simpson had never lived; let alone died. What I wrote in my diary that day will I hope explain what I feel his legacy to be.

Friday 13 July 2007

I don't think it is right that 90 per cent of the peloton today will not have been aware that it was the fortieth anniversary of Tommy Simpson's death. We can't forget that day or that rider. Our sport is finally facing up to the fundamental problems it has. The culture of doping that was omnipresent for years is finally being eradicated, but only because we are in an end-game situation where if we don't face it we'll all be out of jobs. That's the bottom line: it's the economic factors that are forcing people to act. I believe we can do better than that. I believe we can bring real ethics and sportsmanship back into our beautiful sport. It is going to take time, but the next generation deserves never to have to face the same decisions that generations of cyclists have faced at one time or another. We can only give the future a proper chance if we face up to the past and deal with it, hear from the experiences of people, the hows and whys of doping in cycling. Otherwise we'll forget, and years from now it will happen all over again.

Three years ago, Paris drug police arrested me in a restaurant in Biarritz. I spent the following forty-eight hours in a cell intermittently being interrogated, and I remember lying there in a sleepless state wondering what the hell had happened to the teenager who dreamed of one day winning the Tour de France. Ten years before I had a bedroom covered in cycling posters and an absolute love for the sport. Now I was lying on a wooden bench in a French prison for doping and – worst of all – I'd grown to hate cycling. That's what happened to me and so many others. We cheated and lied and grew to hate the one thing we'd loved above all else in our youth. My story is important; so is Tommy Simpson's; so is Marco Pantani's; so is

'Chava' Jiménez's; so is Festina's, so is Cofidis'; so is Telekom's; so is Operacíon Puerto's. The list goes on and on and on.

The future is good though. I love what I do with an awareness which can only come from loss. I know we'd be absolutely fine if everybody could see through my eyes for a day, but unfortunately that's not going to happen – hence my near-evangelical preaching at times. The sport is going to change infinitely over the next ten years, and the young guys coming in now are getting the ride that we should have all always had the chance at. Next year, a new venture in American cycling will see the first of what will be a fresh generation of cycling teams, bringing ethics back to the forefront. And maybe one day, years from now, cycling will come full circle and stand at the vanguard of international sport when it comes to anti-doping and sportsmanship. That would be a lovely bit of irony, wouldn't it?

As for Tommy, I will continue to doff my helmet /cap to his monument whenever I pass it on the Ventoux, in remembrance of a great cyclist.

That was written two years ago. In the meantime, British cycling has reached new heights, dominating the Olympics in Beijing, seeing membership of its national federation reach record-breaking levels, winning the major prizes at the BBC Sports Personality Awards, and discovering and nurturing one of the greatest sprinters in the sport in Mark Cavendish (the first Brit to win a Classic since Tommy). By next year there will be a leading British professional Tour de France team.

It is important that we remember our roots during all this success and progress, and although Tommy Simpson is not here to share his experiences and entertain us with his stories, I think that we should make the effort to learn about him, the good, the bad and the ugly. Because it's only by knowing Tommy Simpson that we can understand the sport that he and many more love so much. And it is a beautiful sport, even though there is a darkness within it that has existed for far too long. Standing by his monument one kilometre from the top of Mont Ventoux is a moving experience, and only by standing there can we understand how close he got and how far he fell. Tommy Simpson – cycling's very own Icarus.

# The Final Milestone

Tom Simpson's last milestone was reached on 13th July, 1967, on the 13th stage of the Tour de France, just about one kilometre from the summit of Mont Ventoux, the 'Giant of Provence'. He died in the saddle, exhausted and asphyxiated by the combination of effort, altitude and heat.

He was never a strong man in a physical sense which made his feats all the more remarkable. Thin and not very muscular around the shoulders or the chest, it was, to look at him, impossible to tell from where he obtained his powers of endurance and energy.

What was it then that drove this great man to his death? Ambition? Money? Vanity? These are three things which motivate people to push themselves harder than ever before but, knowing him as I did, it certainly was not the latter. Ambition could have been his downfall in this case, particularly with the Tour de France because he had always wanted to win it.

Perhaps, though, it was the money. He had a burning desire to make enough so that he could retire early and enjoy life with his wife and two daughters. He had suffered badly financially when he broke his leg in a skiing accident in January, 1966, for he lost an enormous amount of good contract money which, as the then reigning world champion, could have meant something in the region of £30,000.

After a short holiday over Christmas in 1966 he concentrated on trying to make up the deficit of that unlucky year and, like all the other bad times when he was so often dogged with ill-luck and misfortune, he came bouncing back with all his old fire and enthusiasm.

I think he overdid his racing in his efforts to get back to the top and earn more money to ensure a happy time was ahead for him and his family when he 'hung up his wheels' for the last time. But it was not avarice that killed him, he was never a greedy man and I feel it was the combination of wanting, so desperately to regain his position in the racing world after that bad season and to prove his world title was no fluke, that he went all out to ride and try to win everything he rode.

He competed in several Six Day events before launching himself into the road season. He won a stage in the Tour of Sardinia, was the overall winner of the eight stage, Paris-Nice classic and then went on to win two stages of the Tour of Spain, the latter event saw him crash badly but come back into the fight once more. In between these events he raced in many minor races all over Europe, flogging his thin frame one day and then driving perhaps six, seven, or even eight hundred miles to ride somewhere else the next day.

He spoke French like a Frenchman, lived in Belgium, raced mainly abroad but remained British to the core throughout, always proud of it and never forgetting to remind the Continentals of it. He had to 'have a go', that was his way and nobody could change him. It was this attitude, his determination, his doggedness and his will to win, these qualities emerging more and more in times of adversity, that ended his career so tragically.

When he fell from his machine on Mont Ventoux on that fateful day he did what one could only have expected. He asked to be put back on his bike. He was then at death's door but still would not give in. He was still in possession of all his faculties for he recognised people and spoke to them by name but, as he weaved drunkenly across the road for the last time and was held up by spectators, he had reached the end of the road, his final milestone. Eye-witnesses told me that his fingers had to be prised from the handlebars and it took two helpers to open his mouth, so tightly clenched were his teeth, before they could lay him down at the roadside and administer the 'kiss of life' and oxygen, neither remedy having any effect.

Thus, the Tour de France beat him in the end as it had done on all but three occasions in his racing life. This time though, it was the supreme sacrifice but he went the way I think he would have liked to have done, spectacularly. And, if it was just to be the first man to die in the Tour de France, then it was another Simpson achievement which he would have grinned about.

Ironically enough, the British press had a field day when he died, giving front page treatment in almost every case. The majority had rarely bothered to give coverage to his many victories which earned him a reputation which travelled even further than the continent of Europe.

We were friends for some years and I had a wonderful time with him when we prepared this book. It had been agreed that after he retired we would write another together, one in which things could be said that would have been impossible to record in this one. It was to have been entitled, 'Cycling Was My Life' . . .

I do not have to write about the sort of person Tom

Simpson was, it shows itself pretty plainly in the pages of this book.

There may be other British riders who will achieve similar honours in the years to come but it will be difficult for them to live up to his personality, his charm and his humour.

British sport and international cycling lost one of its greatest men on 13th July, 1967. It will be very, very hard, in fact impossible, to replace him.

*David Saunders*, 1967.

# The First Milestones

It's strange how when you cast your mind back over by-gone events, the milestones which meant so much at the time seem to blend with one another and the memory becomes hazy. Such things as when you first tasted bacon and eggs or first relaxed in the warm sun you cannot remember at all. Others are vivid and one in particular which is anything but hazy in my mind occurred when I was twelve years old. It was the time I first started riding a bike and that bike was a shocker.

I have four sisters, all older than myself, and the bike belonged to my brother-in-law. It had big pedals, thick tyres and was as far removed from a lightweight racing machine as anything you can imagine. But this didn't matter. I used to push it round the block where we lived in Harworth taking it in turns with my brother Harry, who was two years older than myself, and two cousins. In all, about eight of us used to thrash our way round and each was timed by the others with an ordinary watch. The timing was not very accurate because the watch had no second hand but everyone tried to be fair. In any case, the others would spot it immediately if anyone tried any tricks because everyone watched everybody else's ride round the block and everyone not riding was an unofficial official!

All this happened soon after we had moved to Harworth

from Durham because my father, a miner, had an accident and never went down the pits again. At Harworth, he managed to find a job in a glassworks, but this, of course, is in Nottinghamshire. How I came to be adopted as a York-shireman arose later, probably because much of my early racing was in that county and I later joined a Rotherham club and maybe because they are canny folk in those parts they saw they were on a good prospect, encouraged me and chose me as 'theirs' long before I made any headlines. Any-how, I'm proud they did and hope they are proud of me.

In those early days at Harworth my family did not have much money so, although I was soon longing for a bike of my own once I could ride, the chances of having one were highly improbable. Eventually, I got an old machine for my-self and joined the Harworth District Cycling Club as a tiny lad. At that time I was really small for I did not start to sprout for several years, but they welcomed me to the fold and soon I was riding in my first ever time trial. This was something better than the round-the-houses races against a sometimes faulty watch but I still recall my dismay at record-ing seventeen minutes fifty seconds for five miles. But as the event, an evening affair, was timed by my brother Harry, and especially as he was using a good watch, I could not complain.

Harry was a good all-round sportsman being better than average at cricket, soccer, and riding but he soon tired of riding though I believe he was the fastest in the club when he gave it up. I was not interested in any other games or sport and all I thought about was riding but, my goodness, I soon found that I had a lot to learn. They were good lads in the club and despite my scrawny frame I began to enjoy myself on club nights and club runs.

After a time, I decided that I would have to have a pukka racing machine if I was to keep up with the others. That, I

found, would cost money which, as I have said, was in short
supply so I got myself an evening and week-end job deliver-
ing bread and groceries round the district. For this I received the princely sum of ten shillings a week which I
gave to my mother but received back half a crown for
pocket money. Now and again I managed to pick up a few
tips but was allowed to keep these, so gradually I was able to
save up.

For my rounds I had a bike with a big basket in front
which at times was very heavy, but it was taking me to another milestone so I kept at it. It was when I was on the
bread round that I saw a man riding a lightweight bike to
and from a nearby colliery where he worked. As he lived in a
house where I served bread, I eventually asked him if he
would swop my own bike for his. As I look back, I must have
been a bit cheeky in those days—maybe I still am—but I
knew what I wanted and was never embarrassed in asking for it. By this time I had spent some of my money on
paint and had renovated my old 'un so that it shone a nice
bright pillar-box red. I must have asked a dozen people if
they would exchange their bikes for it and, not surprisingly,
they said nothing doing. Eventually, the colliery man must
have become fed up with my pleas, gave in and the swop
was made.

It wasn't a complete racing bike but by the time I had
got some other pedals and a single fixed wheel it was good
enough for my immediate requirements and I was all set.
Just wait till I get to the club, I thought, I'll screw 'em down,
but it wasn't as easy as that. Even with the right tools, I
could not do the job properly because I was too small.

As a trier, I got plenty of encouragement and the members
made me feel popular but on club runs they gave me no
quarter. For example, they often went to Cleethorpes and
back on a Sunday going one route and returning via Market

Rasen. This was a run of just over a hundred miles with some hills that would see me off. On the long drags I would be left behind and come puffing into Cleethorpes just as they would be starting back after a rest and cup of tea. This meant an immediate turn round for me and I would keep with them on the flat but the hills would soon see me at the rear again.

The only prize I got was the nickname Four-stone Coppi, partly because I was so scrawny that I looked as if I weighed no more than four stone and partly after Fausti Coppi, the great Italian champion. I was very proud of that nickname and it helped keep me going. As time went on I improved until the great day arrived when I was sixteen and I won the club 25-mile time trial. My time was just over the hour and the success went straight to my head which became, so to speak, as big as the rest of my body. I felt like a hero and recall shouting the odds about my victory round the clubroom to a lot of unsmiling faces. My bragging did not go down at all well for I had beaten a lot of older riders and eventually I got the slap-down I had been asking for. Presently, during a pause there came a voice from somewhere in the room saying pointedly, 'Little stars don't shine bright for long.' After that, it was never the same any more somehow, and I became very miserable.

For the next few days I did a lot of thinking about it and eventually came to the conclusion that I would have to find another club. I had to do so for two reasons. One was that the sky was now the limit for I was sure that I would soon be able to beat anyone in my present club so I had to find a club where I was a rabbit again and try to beat the other members and the other reason, equally important to me, was I wasn't as popular any more. The clubmen didn't encourage me any more, as if they resented me winning. Now I know that it wasn't the winning they resented, but my bragging about it, but all the same I couldn't stand it. Even today I like to be liked and to be accepted by other people, not because I might be somebody special but just to be able to talk and joke with folk and share a laugh. Milestones have meant a lot in my life, but so too have friendships. You leave milestones behind you, but not your friends. The winning of the time trial at Harworth was another milestone in more senses than one and I have never really forgotten it. They say he travels furthest who travels alone, but even the best can do with a pace-setter at times. If you are riding to win, you eventually leave him behind but when the race is over you wait around to thank him. So although I was unhappy when I left Harworth, I have never really forgotten how much I owe them.

# 2

# Digging the Foundations Deep

BY NOW I had left school and was working as an apprentice draughtsman at a factory in Retford, about ten miles from home. This meant more pocket money for me—and my bike, of course—and I enjoyed the ride to and from work, treating it as good training. Road racing had always had a great attraction for me and there were occasions when I had even played truant from school to see the riders pass in the Tour of Britain when it was anywhere in the area. I would also visit Nottingham as often as possible at week-ends to watch the circuit racing in the Forest Recreation Ground where I would stand goggle-eyed to gaze at my heroes, Brian Robinson, Bob Maitland, 'Tiny' Thomas and others, dreaming of the day when I would be like them. On occasions I would even ride the fifty miles to Scarborough to see my idols.

Meanwhile, while working at Retford although I did not own a track bike I had my first taste of track racing. This was at Blythe on what was, in fact, a grass track where I did very well considering I was a novice at that type of riding.

I just took the brakes off my road machine hoping that this would do but it caused a lot of argument among the officials and competitors because the ordinary alloys I had were not really suitable. Some of the riders said they would not compete if I rode with this machine and I don't know what would have happened if Eric Gordon, a Birmingham rider, hadn't been kind enough to loan me a pair of proper wheels for the track.

Anyhow, I had a go and managed to get through various heats and into four separate finals. I came unstuck here but managed to get third place in the half mile. It was entirely different from what I had imagined and while I continued for a time to ride the tracks, both grass and cement, I longed for road racing.

As I mentioned, I wanted to leave the Harworth club and about this time I joined the Scala Wheelers, a Rotherham club, and I soon found I got on very well with all the members. They included some very good riders and I thoroughly enjoyed the time trials and club runs which they organised, for they were a grand crowd.

By now, I had started to grow and shot up six inches in as many months. In addition, I filled out and, accordingly, began to ride better and faster. It wasn't long before I was able to satisfy my ambition and enter for my first road race. This was as a junior rider and, by a coincidence, on the Forest circuit at Nottingham where I used to watch the stars. I shall remember that day for a long time because I dropped into the style or tactics which I have used virtually ever since.

I don't recall how many laps we had to do or the total distance but I think it was about twenty miles. As we massed together for the start, I said to myself, 'There's only one way to win this race—from the front!' so I went straight off into the lead and stayed there for lap after lap. It was hard going with a steep climb on every lap but I stuck to my guns. Things seemed very promising until the last lap and then something happened that was to happen many times in my career as a professional—I was caught. I was overtaken in the sprint and had to be content with second place. Natur-

ally, I was very disappointed but nevertheless, I thought I
had done a fabulous ride—until a little later.

Soon afterwards, I was at Lincoln to see the finish of a
stage of the Tour of Britain and fell into conversation
with a group of other cyclists. We were near the finishing
line and were gassing generally about racing when the talk
turned to tactics. One of the fellows was expounding his own
theories on how to win races and said, 'You can't win from
t'front. You've to bide your time and wait for t' sprint. Look
at that daft bloke at Nottingham t'other week. He went off
like a madman and what happened? He got caught.' And
there was no mistaking what he thought about the rider.
'Did you see him, Charlie?' he asked one of his mates and
it was clear that Charlie shared the same view. And then he
turned to me and asked if I had seen him.

What could I say, for I was the daftie they were talking
about. As they had seen the event, I thought they would
have at least recognised me, so rather embarrassed, I mut-
tered that I hadn't seen him. There may have been something in what they were saying but not for me and I often
wonder what they would have said if they knew that the
object of their scorn became a world champion.

During the following year, my seventeenth, I continued
to grow and improve my riding and won sixteen races—all
from the front! They were junior races and soon I began to
receive some recognition, the effect being that I was not
allowed to ride in some junior races any more. I managed to
win the junior hill climb championship but began to spend
more time on the tracks where, in the same year, I won the
area championship on the red shale track at Brodsworth,
near Doncaster.

By now, everything about cycling mattered to me and I
read avidly every magazine or book I could put my hands on
if it had anything about the sport. If it had any suggestions

about seat position, gears, sprinting, diet or anything else, I tried it. I tried the lot. I even wrote letters to past champions or anyone else I thought could give any help or advice. Not all the information and tips that came back was useful but I read all the replies carefully and benefited tremendously.

One of those I contacted was George Berger, the naturalised Englishman, who had ridden in France for many years with the Velo Club, Lavallois. He had been trained by Paul Rouinart, a famous Directeur Sportif, and really knew a lot about the game. We wrote enormously long letters to each other and by the time I met him nearly two years later, he had influenced me enormously by his thinking and his advice.

Berger played a great part in steadying and guiding me along the dedicated road that is necessary to be a good professional rider. I shall always remember him writing to me about the necessity of preparation, of mental training and never being satisfied by performances but, at the same time, never to worry over them. He would say that they were only a part of the training for bigger things. He put it quite easily in the phrase, 'the deeper the foundations, the higher the building' and I was inspired by his philosophy.

I read and re-read his letters and became absorbed in his views. Anything but cycling had to be ignored, for there could be no distractions from the straight line to becoming a class rider. He translated a number of French books on training for me and, in all, gave me advice for a period of about four years. He made me decide that today was not important nor, really, were the achievements then—they were only the preliminaries to much greater things.

This mental fitness and self-discipline came to be, perhaps, my greatest asset in my early years as a professional. I am inclined to be impulsive at times and, even when I have

gone off the deep end as it were, this advice from George
Berger has always steadied me and prevented me from giving up. There are many, many occasions in the life of a professional roadman when he wants to stop and throw his bike
over a hedge and many times it was sheer will-power that
kept me on the road. I could never have survived the rigours
of continental racing without this mental toughness and, of
course, having accepted the advice as a very young man, it
was not so difficult to keep on the straight and narrow later
on. It is as if the right habits become second nature as you
become older.

During this period, and even when I had started cycling,
a battle had begun in England over road racing. The
National Cyclists Union were the governing body of cycle
sport in the country and they did not permit racing on the
open roads. In the 1940's a new group had been formed, the
British League of Racing Cyclists, whose sole object in
life was to promote this side of the sport and they had, over
the years, made quite an impression. The B.L.R.C., despite
the N.C.U. banning riders and officials for life, progressed
and there were many bitter arguments about things.

Perhaps because of this, but not entirely, I was suspended
for six months when I was still a junior rider. The two war-
ring parties in the sport had come to an agreement on the
question of suspensions if a road rider committed any
offence under the Road Traffic Act. Thus my own impetu-
osity became my downfall for, while on another lone break,
I did not stop at a 'halt' sign and was caught by the
police. That was the end of that race and very nearly my
career

It was a hard blow for me to stomach after all the trials,
the training, the efforts and the sacrifice, to be denied my
chosen sport. I was very bitter about it all and decided to
take up motor cycle trials. I had had a motor bike and rather

fancied myself with it, but I rode it very much as I did my push-bike and eventually it all but fell to pieces! On one occasion when I drove down to watch a trials event, I had an old sidecar and, clever as usual, roared it into the event car park, throttle, brakes, the lot. The sidecar immediately parted company and continued on its own across the field but luckily no one was in the way. I always had to get the maximum out of everything and I had taken that poor old bone-shaker beyond its normal capacity and loosened nearly every nut and bolt!

I had my eye on a D.O.T. trials machine but, the usual problem, I could not afford it. So I decided to sell my bike which, by now, was quite good and put it on the market for the princely sum of £25. That plus the £75 I had was the price of the D.O.T. but the nearest offer I got was £20. I just couldn't let it go for that and persevered in my attempts to gain the money I needed. I didn't make it and took so long in trying that the six months were over and I could ride again.

A couple of years later, in 1958, the war between the two sides ended when they amalgamated into the present British Cycling Federation. It came only just in time, because the sport very nearly died with all the petty rules and restrictions that came of it. Everyone who rode events during the troubles had to have two licences, a separate one being issued by each body, and there must have been dozens of first class riders lost to the sport each year.

While I still loved road racing, I turned my attention to the track, mainly because of what George Berger had said. He maintained that one should try to model one's self on a great rider, much as the cricket coaches try to get their protégés to follow the style of famous batsmen. I was trying to emulate the late Swiss champion, Hugo Koblet. He was known in his racing days as the *pedaleur du charme* and it was a sad blow to all cycling when he was killed in a road accident in 1965.

Berger had said that pursuiting might well be a good thing for me to take up. Many of the champions had done so and I concentrated on this particular aspect of the sport. It so happened that Britain had a number of really good pursuiters at that time; in fact they were considered to be very much world class. We were, without doubt, in the middle fifties, one of the most feared nations in this section of the track sport.

With so many in the top bracket I had to meet the challenge and, in preparing for the 1958 National Individual Pursuit title, I met another man who was to make a very important impression upon me, Cyril Cartwright.

# 3

# In Search of Medals

I MET Cyril Cartwright at Fallowfield about three weeks before the title race in 1956. He told me that I could win the Pursuit Championship if I cared to listen to what he said. Naturally I was keen to do so and moved to his home in Ashton-under-Lyme for the remaining fortnight.

He was a most remarkable man and, like Berger, created a tremendous enthusiasm inside me for the sport. Everything was changed now. All the things I had learnt as a roadman were altered. My seat position, methods of training, work-outs and, a thing in which Cyril had great faith, special dieting.

He taught me an awful lot about food, what to eat and what to leave alone. While meat was taken in fairly normal quantities the emphasis was on fresh fruit and salads and their juices. Extracts of juices from raw vegetables and fruit were a big thing as were salads which had nuts and grated carrots and the lot. It was his theory that by eliminating certain toxins, present in various foods, the body would have less work to do in digesting meals.

I was also lectured on nature cures and how to fast so that impurities would leave the body. I suppose you think he was a bit of a crank, but you have never been more mistaken, believe me. Cyril Cartwright had rheumatic fever in 1948. He was in agony for a long time and lost so much

weight that he looked like a Belsen inmate. There was
nothing, the doctors said, that could be done for him and he
was virtually at death's door. He was given some of these
nature cures and slowly but surely regained his health. So
much so, and this is why I haven't told you before, that he
took second place in the World Pursuit Championship the
following year, 1949.

Who was I to argue with him over these theories? He was
wonderful the way he took me under his wing and literally
built me up both physically and mentally for the championship. He gave me his machine that he had ridden for his
world's silver medal and arranged for me to train at Fallowfield with the great Reg Harris. Harris was still terrifically
strong and he, too, gave me considerable help. Cyril, though,
gave me confidence in myself just as Berger had done.
Between them they convinced me that I was good and that
one day I would prove that no one was better.

So the scene was set for my first, properly prepared championship and I felt great. Inside me was an ever-growing
feeling of confidence that I could win. By the morning of the
title race I was quite determined that no-one could beat me
for I had something of a psychological advantage over the
others in that I had trained better than they had. I must
admit to slight feelings of doubt when I thought of Norman
Shiel and Pete Brotherton, two of the men that I would be
up against, for they had taken first and second place re-
spectively in the World Championship the previous year.

I had also begun to realise that pursuiting over the re-
quired distance of 4,000 metres suited me, particularly mentally, and that George Berger was right. It is a very
strenuous business, taxing both muscle and brain, and if
you are just a fraction down on your opponent it needs iron
nerves and firm control to keep going without overdoing
things before the end.

Fallowfield track had its usual crowd who, although they didn't know it then, were swarming into the stadium to witness one of the finest pursuit championship battles ever to be staged in Britain. I was, by now, having some slight attacks of butterflies in the stomach and found it difficult to concentrate.

Everything turned out all right as the time drew near and my first ride was against Brotherton. I beat him after a tussle and then went through to the quarter finals where I was up against the reigning world champion, Norman Shiel. There was no stopping now, I had all the confidence in the world and took the match easily going into the semi-final with big John Geddes from Liverpool.

This was a close ride! We both went from the gun and there was nothing in it all the way round for lap after lap. On the final circuit I managed to just get in front and beat him by only a tenth of a second, recording 5 minutes 10 seconds for the distance, the fastest time then ever recorded at Fallowfield.

While resting before the final where I was up against Mike Gambrill of the Clarence Wheelers—a London club, I got a bit unnerved when a Liverpudlian supporter threatened to knock my head off for beating Geddes! I was still jittery as we came to the line but got off to a good start. As we went round on the third lap I punctured and the pursuit was stopped.

As we got ready for the re-run I began to tremble a bit and it took all I had to try and stay calm. Off we went once more and, approaching the halfway mark, Gambrill led me by a fraction as I looked for him on the opposite side of the track. Suddenly I punctured again. Another re-run! I just couldn't take it any more and broke down in tears. That was the end of me and I tried and tried to get on terms with

Gambrill on that third attempt but it was no use, I had to be content with second place.

For a little while I was very miserable and upset but I think Cyril was terribly disappointed. I had got over it by the time I reached home but my parents were also rather disappointed. I think it was for my sake, for I don't imagine they would have worried really if it was merely a question of an honour for the family.

It's a funny thing but when something has gone wrong and you feel a bit cross about it you always tend to take it out on the people who are your nearest and sometimes dearest friends and relatives. I certainly hadn't intended taking it out on my parents but I was a bit snappy. My mother had a smashing tea ready for me and put down the plate in front of me, laden with lovely golden-brown chips. 'You can take those off!' I said, sharply, pushing the plate across the table. Boy! Didn't I get a telling off! The final remark from Mother really brought me down to earth though. 'Don't get on at me! D'you want me to ride your ruddy bike for you?'

Everything settled down all right as they do in the best homes, but I had meant what I had said about not having chips. After my stay with Cyril Cartwright I had to continue with salads and vegetable juices and, as these were expensive, poor Mother had to go out to work again after spending thirty years as a housewife. Occasionally I would have a good blow out with a nice steak but I kept reasonably strictly to the diet.

My father suffered too, poor chap. He usually came home from work to find me tucking into a steak while stew was his supper! They were both wonderful at putting up with my crazy ways and they stood it all magnificently. At least they knew when I went out that I wasn't going to the pub or standing on the street corners and they used to get their own back when I would come in after an evening training ride.

When I had had a bath I would come down and sit in my dressing gown watching television with them. If there was something good on I always had to ask what time it finished. They would chuckle and say it ended at half past nine or later. This was past my bedtime as I drilled myself severely and was religiously between the sheets by nine o'clock every night. I am sure it did me good physically but it was equally beneficial to me mentally and was all part of the self-discipline plan.

I was now riding well on the track and, for a time, the road was forgotten. I saw Cyril at fairly regular intervals now and he was trying urgently to get me chosen for the world championships in September. I was now working as a draughtsman at the glass factory in Harworth where my father was and thus much nearer home so that I had better opportunity for training runs.

Various track promoters were happy to have me compete now because my name had got round quite a bit but I was soon in trouble over my expenses. Both Berger and Cartwright had told me never to cheapen myself and so I always asked for rather high expenses. I did not get them though! It was usually a black look and the normal travelling allowance.

Soon the news came through that I had not been selected for the 'worlds' but had been chosen for the Oympic Games in Melbourne, Australia. Cyril was very angry about it but for me, well, I was delighted at being chosen for the Games and found out very soon afterwards that I was going with the Olympic team to Russia for a number of international matches there against them and the Italians.

This was to be at the middle of September and we would fly out to Russia for about two weeks. I had never been out of England before and, coupled with the chance of riding against the Russian and Italian Olympic teams, I was very

excited and the time passed quickly. My firm had given me
the time off to go and were also good enough to let me off
for the Olympics too, so everything was ready.

There was seven of us in the party, Eric Thompson, Alan
Dawson, Don Burgess, Mike Gambrill, Pete Brotherton,
John Geddes and myself with our Manager, Benny Foster.
We flew first to Leningrad to race there at the stadium, the
like of which I have never seen, before or since.

The Russians were wonderful to us and we were en-
sconced in what was, at one time, a palace. It was a marvellous place with gorgeous rooms and we were given the
most palatial accommodation possible. I had my own bedroom and private bathroom plus another drawing room
but it was Geddes and Dawson who were the kings. They
had a complete suite of five rooms including a bathroom big
enough for a football team. There were waiters everywhere
and trays of caviare all over the place.

Funnily enough we did not eat any! I had a taste but did
not like it and neither did anyone else. We were taken on
sight-seeing trips round the city and it was on one of these
that I was christened. We were down by the river and lark-
ing about a bit and Geddes and Thompson grabbed me and
dipped my backside in the water. It was all good, clean fun
and, with a lot of serious racing to do, there were times
when we had to let off steam.

The Russians did not like it though and sent a letter to
poor Benny. It was from their Cycling Federation and went
on about bad behaviour by the British cyclists. It really was a
sharp note and, as I remember it, said something about 'the
use of superior force on a younger rider', 'senior riders
should know better' etc., etc. Benny, who was a terrific
manager, got cross about it naturally and we all got a good
telling off. He had a very difficult job with us for I think
we were all rather more than boisterous on that trip.

The Leningrad Stadium was fabulous. The track had
been cemented with such care that it was as smooth as
marble and wonderful to ride on. The crowds were enormous and most appreciative considering we beat their own
riders!

.  The racing there was very good and the fact that we came
out on top did us all an awful lot of good. The training
facilities had been excellent for special buses called for us at
our palace every day to take us along to the track.

What, perhaps, had been our chief aid in winning was our
Manager, Benny Foster. He just seemed to know what the
opposition would do and gave us all some pretty good
advice. We had suffered at his hands, or rather his tongue,
but nothing was too much for him to ask of us. In the next
chapter you will find out a little more of Benny which put
him even higher in our estimation if that was possible.

# 4

# First Taste of Success

NEXT we went to Moscow, this time by train and again to a great reception with another good hotel, though not like that in Leningrad. The Russians provided small buses to take us on tours of the city but would not, of course, let us out on our own. We tried several times to lose our guide but couldn't. In between racing we visited Red Square and the Kremlin and saw Lenin's tomb. In the museum there they had some of the clothing worn by Ivan the Terrible. Heck! He must have been a hell of a size because the boots were about three and a half feet high! They also had some of his shirts hanging up. Shirts! That piece of cloth would have made a small tent for somebody.

Talking of that particular item of men's wear reminds me that we met some of the members of one of England's big symphony orchestras staying at our hotel and playing in Moscow. One of them, a funny little chap who had a lisp, just to make things more comical, told us that the male students would do anything for good clothes. He said, 'They'll let you take their girl-friends out if you give them a th-yert. Trouble is, ith tho cold there you can't go out without your th-yert.' This gave us quite a laugh and we lasted on 'th-yerts' for a long time.

He was quite right about it being cold. It was really an icy wind that blew the day we rode against the other Olym-

pic squads. The wind whistled round the track, another good
one by the way, and we were thinking about lowering our
gearing because of it. Benny would have none of it and, in
fact, made us go up! We had on average an 86° gear and he
pushed us up to 92. We thought at first it was crazy but we
had such faith in him that none of us really doubted his
word. The Italians had dropped their gearings but as soon
as we went out into the wind, pushing the bigger one round
was a great help for it stopped a lot of wobbling, especially
on the bankings. So it was another triumph for Benny
and we were sorry to see him go a few days later after we had
been invited to compete in Sofia in Bulgaria. The British
Federation agreed since our expenses would be paid but we
had to travel without Benny who, owing to business, had to
fly back to London.

Before we left Moscow we were entertained by the Russian Federation at the Bolshoi Theatre where we were
given a feast of opera and ballet, and the following day,
taken to a football match between Russia and Hungary. I
remember most that the snow came down steadily and that
we were just about frozen for it was a boring game with nothing to shout about. That, at least, was my reaction but I do
not really consider football to be a sport anyhow. It is just
a game and I just don't seem to enjoy it. This, funnily
enough, is despite the fact that my brother Harry was a
professional footballer for some years and, at one time,
played for Blackpool.

When we left Moscow by train for Sofia there was an
unexplained happening which had us in a bit of a state
and, in spite of all the kindness we received on our journeys
behind the Iron Curtain, there was always the feeling that
one of us could disappear without causing too much fuss or
concern in the neighbourhood.

We had been picked up at our hotel and taken by bus to

the station. That is to say, all of us except Pete Brotherton who, for reasons best known to the officials, was taken in one of their cars. We reached the railway station and boarded the train, carefully shepherded by the officials who came with us. The usual farewells were made and then we were left sitting. Suddenly, the train moved out. No Brotherton. Well, we all thought, here's a fine kettle of fish. And it was too, believe me. There we were, six Englishmen, complete with bikes and luggage but with no tickets and travelling heaven-knows-where in pitch dark, unable to speak the language and one member of the party missing.

One of us had a small map of Europe and we tried vainly to estimate our position and direction by that and the stars. After an hour's steady grind through the night and with everyone in the compartment trying to plot our course, we came to the opinion that we were all heading for Siberia. There were a number of jokes by various older companions but nobody laughed very much and, when nearly two hours had passed, I was beginning to get positively frightened.

Quite suddenly the train stopped, apparently in a field for all we could see. There were sounds of voices, and then Brotherton appeared on board. Were we pleased to see him! He had no idea that anything was wrong and explained he had been taken along to the official's home to meet his wife and then brought out to catch the train. There never was any further explanation but somehow I felt that it was not a mistake and the Russians were just showing us boisterous Britishers who was boss!

That was not the end of our troubles by a long chalk for we had to pass through Rumania to get into Bulgaria and, just after we had crossed the frontier, the train stopped at a station where we all had to get out. It appeared that we had no visas to enter that particular country and were placed under arrest. We did not mind getting off since we had been stuck on that train for over twenty-four hours and being able to stretch our legs was a relief. Eventually we were put on another train which took us into Bucharest where we were whisked off to the British Consulate and placed under house arrest for twenty-four hours. Eventually, everything was sorted out and, a day and a half late, we continued our journey and arrived, not much the worse for wear, in Sofia.

The treatment was much the same as before. We had first class hotels and plenty of food but rarely were we allowed out on our own. The racing was good and we showed up well again in front of large, enthusiastic crowds. I was not sorry though to get back home and spent a marvellous few days telling everyone about Russia, about being arrested and about all that had happened.

Being away for so long, I had not been able to get fitted for my Melbourne uniform and was obliged to take a trip to London to be measured for my blazer, etc. I decided I would ride down thinking it would be good training for me and arranged to stay for the night with my sister Alice, who lives at Mill Hill.

After lunch on a Friday, I set off. I was very fit of course and the ride did not seem to do me any harm, for I covered the one hundred and sixty miles in about eight hours and felt none the worse for wear. I cheated a bit at times down the A.1 for I tucked in behind a few lorries and took pace! On the Saturday morning I was fitted up and then turned the bike round to head for the Great North Road.

On that ride back I took a hammering. I stopped several times for a bite to eat and a drink, but began to realise that I was only kidding myself that I was hungry. What I really needed was rest. Eventually, when I reached Grantham I had had enough and rode to the station and caught the train

home. I remembered then that as a very young lad of about
twelve when I had my first bike, I did about sixty miles. It
took about fourteen hours and on reaching home I vowed
I would never go over any such distance until I knew what
was what. This time it was too much for me and I was well
and truly shattered. A good training ride indeed! I reckon,
looking back on it, I must have been stark, staring bonkers!

The great day soon arrived and we flew first to Singapore where we stayed for a day. We put up at the famous
Raffles Hotel and as we had been on the 'plane for nearly
two days we wanted to get out to see the sights. We managed
to dodge our manager, Benny Foster, by nipping out the
back way and cramming into a large rickshaw. I forget the
name of the area we were not supposed to visit but we went
straight there! There was not much really to see but we were
pretty lucky because the Singapore riots had only just died
down. We could easily have been involved in a stone-throw-
ing and fighting 'do' and so were very fortunate to get
away with things.

I had my first taste of Asiatic bargaining there in one of
the street markets with a small Chinaman who appeared to
me from my six feet to be about two feet high. I wanted to
buy a pair of shorts and a shirt and he started off at four
pounds but gradually I got him down to five bob! Not
content with that, he produced some Communist China
stamps for which he wanted fifty dollars but yours truly told
him I only had a few shillings left. So he let me have the
stamps too!

Off then to Darwin where it was boiling hot and thence
to Sydney and a good look at Bondi Beach before moving on
to Melbourne and the Olympic Village. What a fantastic
place! It really was out of this world. Each team had its own
bungalow and I shared a room with one of the road team
members, Bill Holmes of Hull. The food was wonderful

and we used to drink such enormous quantities of fresh fruit juice that it got round that the cyclists were gluttons for it and we had to be rationed! The restaurant, too, was quite fabulous with just about every kind of food imaginable. There were at least eighteen different types of breakfast cereal so there was no question of meals lacking variety.

Our first taste of Australian tracks was at Geelong, about fifty miles distant where we were driven by Benny, who had a special van for us. I was not very impressed by either the track which was, I swear, about six hundred yards round, or the racing. Later, we went to ride a track at Essenden, some twenty miles from the Olympic Village, and this was quite a different story. Here the track was only about two hundred metres and made of boards painted white which went across the track against the run of the riders. They were all bolted down but were loose to allow some play because of the heat. The noise, when about twenty riders were hitting the bankings, sounded like that of a motor cycle race and really built up excitement. It was a wonderful, exhilarating experience to see the colour of the jerseys against the white background of the track, to hear the noise of the boards rattling and of the enthusiastic roaring of the crowds.

We had about two weeks there at Melbourne before our big day arrived and used to train on the track in the stadium but first thing in the morning was always a road run in the locality supervised by Benny who kept up with us on a motor scooter. He wanted to be sure that nobody shirked and kept a watchful eye over us in case anyone disappeared into the town.

During these rides, which were over roads where a new housing estate was being built, I found a short cut between some already occupied houses and two of the roads. I also found out that in one of these houses lived a great big dog

which threatened to have some part of one's anatomy if he
was disturbed. I decided that Benny should try our quick
way through and one morning, having told the others, I
shouted 'This way, Benny!' disappearing off the road and
through this narrow gap. It was very tiny and bumpy and
just wide enough for a bike to get through and as I raced by
the house I yelled for the dog. Right on cue he growled out
into the pathway just as Benny belted into the opening and
immediately got stuck in one of the holes in the path! Poor
Benny! We stood there and nearly cried with laughter at
the sight of him wrestling with the scooter and trying to keep
clear of the dog which leapt all around him, barking like
mad. He forgave us though and I think got some amusement out of it himself.

The day came for the Opening Ceremony and what an
impressive affair it was. I was eighteen and it was the greatest moment of my life up till then. It was very emotional as
first the Olympic flame was carried in and then the flags
struck. We cyclists, a cheery mob as always, caused a few
raised eyebrows from other members of the British contingent as we marched in.

I suppose we were wrong to do it, but youth, nerves and
excitement had combined to give all of us a rather mis-
chievous feeling. I am not too sure who started it, possibly
big John Geddes who was always up to various pranks in
those days, but we all punched out our special hats and
shaped them into bowlers. Thus attired, we marched out
and got a special cheer from the Aussies and other Commonwealth people who really appreciated the gag. I am sorry
to say that our attempt at humour was lost upon quite a
few Englishmen who rather thought 'Those damned cycling
chaps let us down'.

Our moment came soon enough and we got ready to do
battle in the semi-final of the team pursuit against Italy.

We all knew that if we beat them a gold medal was ours because the other semi-finalists were France and South Africa, neither team being particularly good. We had already ridden, and won, against the Italians in Russia so we imagined the job we had to do was not very difficult.

But I had a very bad attack of nerves thinking about the gold medals and I am sure, to this day, that I thus lost Britain a great victory. The four man team consisted of Burgess, Geddes, Gambrill and myself, with Gambrill to lead us off on the first half-lap. We had trained mainly to do half a lap each, the front man moving up the banking and tagging on at the back at every half circuit of the track. Benny had said that I could do a full lap if I felt like it, for I was probably the fastest man there, although not the strongest.

My nervousness combined with impulse affected me and when my turn came at the front I did the full lap absolutely flat out. As I swung up the banking at the end of it, I knew I was finished because I was practically asphyxiated through nerves and the tremendous effort I had just put in. When my turn came again I simply could not get enough speed out of myself and I shall always blame myself for the loss of that gold medal, not only for me but for the other members of my team and my country too. It was my impulsiveness which had got the better of me.

The cyclists did not come out of things too badly though, gaining a silver in the road team award and a bronze for the individual third place in the road race plus, of course, our own bronze medal. It was not one of our great years overall and I shall remember for a very long time the effect on me of watching Chris Brasher win the gold in the steeplechase. What a proud moment that was when he mounted the rostrum and they played 'God Save the Queen'. I had witnessed the race, which was terrific, and now, with 80,000

people standing in that vast arena with the strains of the
National Anthem ringing out, the emotion was too much
and I cried. I think also it was because he had, to some degree, compensated for my own short-comings and I felt
much happier.

# 5

# Pride and Fall

I RETURNED from Melbourne about two weeks before
Christmas and, at least, was able to show my bronze medal
to my friends, neighbours and workmates. They were particularly interested for they had all had a 'whip round' so
that I could go as, although my firm let me off for these trips
abroad, I did not get paid when I was away.

Through the winter I should have rested, but no, silly
Simpson decides that he must keep training. I decided that
I must prepare myself for the 1957 World Championship
Pursuit which I, bighead, was going to win. All through
January and February I trained hard, going out every day,
despite the weather, to ride and ride and ride. I do not think
I missed one single day during that period and I just ate,
slept and drank cycling.

During March I started entering time trials at 25 miles
distance and won easily. I was taking something like six
minutes out of the next man home and was very fast indeed.
I probably won nearly every event I entered and had set my
immediate sight on the National '25' at the end of May.

I was reckoned by many people to be the favourite for
the event but nerves got me again on the day. I fell to pieces
and did a terrible ride. I was utterly useless that day and
Norman Shiel won it easily, showing me what preparation
really meant. He had taken his time over his training and

came to the line completely ready for the ordeal. I did not
forget that and realised that I had perhaps begun my efforts
too early.

The following week I was riding in an international omnium at Fallowfield when I crashed badly. I had been off
the bike a number of times before, but this was the worst I
had experienced up to that time. We were riding a points
race and I was just behind a team mate, Johnnie Entwhistle,
with an Italian on my outside as we came round the banking. Johnnie looked back at me and moved out up the banking and I came through on the inside so that the Italian was
blocked. Quite suddenly, as I had filled the space vacated by
Entwhistle, he came down again and 'chopped' across the
front of me. I hit him and so did the Italian and we all fell
heavily on the track.

It felt awful. Sky, earth, crowd, everything went spinning
round and I hit the track all mixed up with my bike. My
left leg was still fastened to the pedal by the toe-strap and
then bent over the cross-bar with me lying across the front
wheel. As the ambulance men and officials lifted me the leg
swelled up to a terrible size and I still do not know how I
did not break it.

I might as well have though, for I was off work for over
four weeks, practically unable to move. The enforced lay-
off did me no good at all for, once I got moving I found I
had lost my speed. Nothing I could do seemed to bring back
my 'snappiness' and it was with reluctance that I entered for
the National Pursuit Championships.

I should not have bothered because I just scraped through
the eliminating round and then was beaten in the quarter
finals. I had lost confidence in myself and was very dejected.
I turned once more to the road and tried my hand at my
old favourite. The races I rode were mainly in the Sheffield
and Derbyshire areas and I managed to gain a little en-

couragement for myself with a number of wins. These were
generally against the independent or semi-professional class
and quite hard, so I was well satisfied with the results.

Towards the end of every season there are a number of
hill climb events culminating in the National Championship. They are really very specialised and often ridden by
men who do little else in other sections of the sport. Quite
often they are won by them too, leaving the normally recognised racing men way behind! There were two such
championships that year. One for the B.L.R.C. and the
other for the time trialists, organised by the R.T.T.C. I went
in for both and won the League event, much to my surprise. Then, at the end of October, I went over to Derbyshire to contest the R.T.T.C. Championship which was
being held at Winnats Pass in the Peaks near Castleton.

I forget now which number I was 'off', but when the time
came the Chief Judge, Pat Shaw, called me up with a
minute to go. I was held on the bike and fixed my feet in the
straps. 'Half a minute!' called the timekeeper, 'ten seconds!'
then Shaw said: 'Mr. Simpson, you have no locking ring
and will be disqualified if you start like that!' I heard the
timekeeper saying 'Five, four, three, two, one!' and jumped
off the bike in a complete fury. How I did not throw it at Mr.
Shaw I shall never know. 'You stupid little nit!' I shouted.
'Just because I won the B.L.R.C. hill climb you want to dis-
qualify me. That's how you go is it? You're too small to bat
anybody and you take it out on them that way!' I called him
all the names I could think of and he just stood there and
took it. As I paused for breath he said: 'Mr. Simpson, if you
calm yourself and find a locking ring you can start.' He was
marvellous and I wished that I had had the same self-
control. I hope Mr. Shaw has since forgiven my outburst.

I rushed off madly to find someone who would lend me
the missing piece of equipment and soon found a rider in the

crowd at the start. Everyone must have heard my outburst,
but feeling not at all ashamed of myself then, I put the ring
on my rear sprocket, muttering all the time 'Ruddy cheek.
Who does he think he is. Nobody else has locking rings on,
why pick on me?' and so on until I had it ready and moved
back to the starting line. It was hopeless now really but I
was determined to have a go. As the timekeeper yelled
'One! Go!' I threw myself up the hill and caught my
minuteman in about five hundred yards and then 'blew up'.
That was that, but only to be expected of me in those nervy,
impulsive days.

I wound down gradually after this and took stock of
things. I decided that I would give the bike a rest and have
a lay-off for a month or so. Apart from a little weight-train-
ing to keep me in trim, I did no riding at all until after January, 1958, had passed. Then I started to ride steadily, taking my time, first over short distances and then gradually
building up the speed and the miles. After only a few weeks
I felt good and knew that I had found all my lost form.

It was back to the track again and more time spent at
Cyril Cartwright's home. I was beginning to 'fly' now and
looked forward to competing in the well-known Good
Friday Meeting at Herne Hill. Unfortunately I asked for too
much in the way of expenses (you know all about that) and
so did not get to London. It did not matter much for there
were plenty of events in the North.

The Whit Monday Meeting at Fallowfield saw me right
on form and I won the Daily Herald Gold Trophy; after
that all sorts of good things started to happen. I was chosen
to ride with Norman Shiel in Bulgaria for a fortnight a few
weeks later and it was obvious from my form that I was a
favourite for the British pursuit title and also for selection for
the Commonwealth Games and the World Championships.

We flew out to Bulgaria and spent a smashing two weeks.

We stayed and raced in Sofia which was known to me from my previous visit, of course. The hotel we stayed at was not so good as previously and we did not receive quite the same doting treatment as before, but I suppose they were getting used to us English!

The track was as good as ever and the weather superb. It was terrifically hot during the day and Norman and I used to go down to the track in the early part of the morning to get our training in before the sun was too high. It was on one of these trips that we had an amusing experience. Walking through to the changing rooms we had to pass the showers and did not know until we got in there that the Bulgarian National women's basket-ball team were getting cleaned up. Shiel says he will never forget the look on my face. I was wearing dark sunglasses and carrying my wheels in one hand and the frame in the other. He said I just did not seem to know what to put down first so that I had a free hand to get my glasses off! We stood there transfixed for about a minute, but it seemed like hours! Then we were spotted and an almighty scream went up and they flew into the various corners and out of sight.

It was a welcome distraction but did not interfere with our riding at all because we both put in excellent performances before some very large crowds. I won the 'Grand Prix of the Union of Physical Culture', a title which was engraved all round the enormous trophy they presented. It really was a monster—over three feet high and it weighed a ton. It was made out of metal of some sort and beaten into shape. We both agreed it had come from a melted down American tank left over from the war and tried desperately to sell it so that we would not have to carry it all the way home, but without success. I was glad in a way and it now holds a position of honour in my parents' house, where Father gives it a bath in soapy water once a month. That

seems to be the only way to clean it because it will not polish
at all!

Our victories in Sofia became well-known and one day
the track had a visit from the British Ambassador himself.
He was very kind to us and actually laid on a special Garden
Party at the Embassy in our honour. That was a wonderful
day and everybody there was so nice it was a pleasure to have
gone out just for that alone. All the Embassy staff seemed
interested in us and what we were aiming for and I often
wonder if they followed our progress over the years.

We left Sofia the day after the party and flew to Borgas
on the Black Sea for a race at the stadium there. It was quite
a small town, obviously being developed, and we were quite
taken by the black sand along the seashore. We had a very
pleasant time swimming and lying on the beach for the short
stay that was allowed us. At first, it was a most peculiar feeling walking on to the beach because it seemed like treading
on coal dust!

The track there was a bit rough but we produced some
good rides again before excellent crowds. I think there was
little else for them to see really and they all flocked in. I
saw my first camel there, not in the stadium, in the town.
They were owned by the Army there though what on earth
they did with them I do not know. The Army visited the
track too and on the big afternoon there we had the whole
back straight filled with troops. There must have been about
two thousand of them and they all made a hell of a noise,
cheering just about everything that happened.

Norman and I thought we would take the 'mickey' out of
them when we were riding our laps of honour, complete with
bouquets of flowers. We rode slowly round and threw single
flowers to the soldiers instead of to the girls. We thought
they would not like it but our plan misfired for they loved it!
Every flower presented was greeted by a great roar of

approval by the whole audience and the soldiers applauded loudest of all, those with the flowers waving them madly.

All good things come to an end and we reluctantly left to return to England via Sofia but not on a very long stop. The time had passed quickly and the friendship that had built up between Norman and I was to break temporarily when we rode against each other in the National Pursuit Championships at Herne Hill.

I did it at last! I took the title easily and was overjoyed to have at last conquered this obstacle. Cyril Cartwright, too, was very pleased but said that I must still concentrate hard on the worlds which were looming up ahead.

Before that, came the Commonwealth Games in Cardiff and here again I fell foul of my own big-headedness and stupidity. I lost the gold by one hundredth of a second to Norman Shiel in a very thrilling match. I started off confidently but Norman was the master tactician on the day, make no mistake about that. He had carefully planned his ride, knowing that I always put in two very fast laps to end the pursuit. I held him all the way round and then, as I began to put the pressure on, I found to my dismay that he was going ahead. I had under-estimated Norman and I could do nothing about it, for he had gone into the lead on the lap before I put on my special burst. With a lap to go I was five seconds down and I almost rode myself into the track trying to pull back the deficit. I thought I had just won at the time, and was still congratulating myself when the decision was announced over the loudspeakers. Talk about pride before a fall! I went down like a pricked balloon and felt very dejected as Norman climbed on to the top rostrum with me below him. I still have a sneaking feeling I just beat Norman, but the judges gave it to him, so that was that!

# 6

# Paris and Beyond

BY NOW I was sure that the World Championship could at last be mine. I had ridden well all the season, the trip to Bulgaria was successful, the National Pursuit title was mine, I had almost won at the Commonwealth Games and had a silver medal. I kidded myself, anyway, that I really won and consoled myself with the fact that it was a moral victory. I was training yet again under the guidance of Cyril Cartwright and was in terrific form. Both physically and mentally I was on top of the world and felt I had only to ride against the others to prove it.

Selection for the 'worlds' was automatic and soon, with the other members of the Great Britain team, I was on my way to Paris for the track events. It was early September and my twenty-first birthday was nearly twelve weeks away. 'A world champion before I am twenty-one,' I thought. Certainly it would be quite an achievement, but I never felt nervous as I had before and never doubted that my prowess was unbeatable. But I did not know what was in store!

We rode at the Parc des Princ track in the French Capital and in the eliminating round I was drawn against the previous world champion, the Italian Simonigh. This was a race against the watch as well as against the other man, for only the eight fastest times would qualify for the quarter-finals. Benny Foster was our Manager once more, and he told me not to exert myself too much on this first run but to pace the Italian carefully and go ahead in the final lap. He knew my last bursts were very fast and that the Italian would be trying hard, so my task was not too difficult.

It was obvious that Simonigh would be going for a good ride and provided I kept him close until the last circuit, I would qualify easily. I really felt good as I sat on the bike looking across the track to the far side where the Italian was receiving his last-minute instructions as he, too, was held on his machine. I eased myself on the saddle, checked the toe-straps and settled into position for the 'off'. The gun went and I was away smoothly, no nerves, no worries, everything was going well.

As we covered the first two thousand metres I had him well in check, and there was little in it between us. Coming up to the bell lap I pushed a bit harder and went ahead: 'Now for it', I thought, and went off on my famous 'flier' round into the back straight. As I took the final banking my front wheel slipped into the narrow guttering that ran just below the track edge. It was still smooth there and I did not realise anything was wrong. As I came out into the final straight, head down and giving everything I had got, I felt the bike start to bump a bit. Looking down I saw the gutter run away down below the level of the trackside and decided that all I need do was jump my front wheel up over the ridge. I was approaching the line fast now—at about thirty to thirty-two miles an hour—and, with fifty yards still to go, pulled the wheel up and on to the track. Just at that point there was a small triangular crack in the edge of the concrete and as my wheel hit it the tyre burst and the front wheel just crumbled beneath me. I saw it suddenly collapse as the line shot by and then, blackness!

I came round in the 'infirmary', a small room in the stadium grandstand. I ached all over and felt sick. My jaw was very painful and I could hardly open my mouth. I found out afterwards that it had been dislocated and put back while I was unconscious. At first I could not remember anything, or why I was there, and then, gradually, everything came back. I got up and went out on to the track where Benny sent me off to our hotel to rest.

Oh! How I ached! Back at the hotel I examined my various injuries. There seemed to be hardly any part of me that did not have a cut or a bruise and I found that a small section of hair had been scraped away just behind my right ear. The officials had said that I had qualified as I had crossed the line before crashing and so was into the next round—the quarter-finals. These were to be held that evening and I was in no fit state to continue. I was sick most of the afternoon, probably from shock, but after a bit of a rest, Benny came into the room.

He said: 'I want you to ride tonight against Dalton.' I was only too ready to have a go but doubted my chances. He said that he was not concerned for me any more because he knew I could not get any further. He was not unkind about it and explained his reasons for wanting me to ride. He said that Dalton might be up against Norman Shiel, who had also qualified that morning, and he did not want Dalton to have a 'ride over' for this would mean that the New Zealander might be fresher. I said the obvious, namely that I would have a crack at it, and Benny told me that I must cover the distance and not retire or the match would be too easy for Dalton.

We got back to the track but when the time came Benny practically had to lift me on my bike. But I was ready to do anything for him. There was no point in my going round for a warm-up—every movement was agony and I was still finding it difficult to speak. 'Don't pack,' said Benny, as he held me at the line ready for the start. 'Make him ride the full distance but don't go and kill yourself!' I mumbled something about being half-dead already and then I was away. Oh! I was so sore! I could not get into any rhythm and just rode round not bothering to look where Dalton was and completed the four thousand metres. Benny helped me off as I crawled in although Dalton had only taken about a quarter of a lap on me. Norman got through to the final where he was up against Gaudrillet, the Frenchman, and took the title without any difficulty at all. While I was delighted with the result I felt very envious as he climbed the victory rostrum. All my trying and training had come to naught and once more I was a failure. I began to feel that fate was against me and I would never do well. I was in despair but after we had returned to England I went over it all again and decided that the crash was entirely my own fault and therefore I had only myself to blame for the whole incident. I knew that had I not fallen I would have won the title. I convinced myself that I was still the best rider in the world, and on the right day I would prove it! I also knew that day was not far away and it would come, if not tomorrow then next week, next month or even next year. Bighead? Perhaps you are right!

I decided that I must turn professional but it was no use trying to get a sponsor until I had done something. I talked to Reg Harris and told him I wanted to have a crack at the World Amateur hour record on an indoor track. He was most helpful and made arrangements for me to have a go in Zürich at the end of November.

Once more I needed time off from work and so went to see the Personnel Manager, Mr. Cowhig. I was a qualified draughtsman now and my journeyings back and forth across the world often meant altered schedules in the firm's drawing office, but he was very nice to me. So I told him of my desire to become a professional rider and he said that if

I wanted I could leave and try my luck. If I succeeded then all was well, but if not, then I was to go back and see him. He told me I could have my job back but must understand that that would be the finish, and if I did return there would be no more rushing off to bike races. No man could have been fairer.

He wished me luck and I set off for Zürich where I found the Track Director, M. Heackler, to be most helpful. I arrived there on the Friday evening and was to ride 'the hour' on the Sunday before the start of a big meeting. The wooden track was really beautiful and very fast, although it had a small ice-rink in the centre which made it very cold. Harris had planned my schedule with me and so I was ready yet again to try to make a name for myself. But another disappointment was due.

My confidence was never better and I was also very fit, but to attack such a record without proper preparatory training was, to say the least, madness. I was undaunted though, and made my effort. I had not had a lot of opportunity to ride the track during my short stay there and the ride itself was to be the longest period I was on it. The cold got into my legs and arms all through the ride and I am sure I could have gone faster if it had been warmer. I covered 43.995 kilometres in the hour, but failed to beat the record by about 300 metres. I was down the drain again! I was disappointed but still not finished.

I packed my bags and took off for Belgium where I went to Ghent and stayed at the Café Den Engel, run by Albert Beurick who I had met briefly at the 'worlds' in Paris. He was kind and, knowing quite a bit about the bike game, was of great assistance to me. He also spoke good English, complete with all the swearwords, and later was to become one of my staunchest supporters and a firm friend.

He got me a ride at the Ghent track where I was up

against a crowd of Belgian amateurs. Well, it was easy! I rode splendidly and lapped the whole field twice to score a convincing win. This, I thought, would set me on the right road and I would get more opportunities to ride there. I was never more mistaken. When Oscar Daemers, the track director, paid me my prize money in his office he told me bluntly that a lot of people had paid good money to come and see their favourites win and not an unknown Englishman. The fact that I beat them so easily made matters worse and he could not give me another ride. He accepted my ability and promised me that if I turned professional and found a partner he would always find me a place in the Six-Days or other events that went on there.

I received 500 francs, for my prize, just enough to pay off my debts and get me home to Harworth. I had a half-a-crown left when I arrived and, as an outwardly beaten man I went back to see Mr. Cowhig. I needed money urgently and took on a labouring job in the factory to work hard and long hours. Every week-end I was at it, getting in the overtime and sometimes working in the furnaces where I drew extra pay, called 'heat money'. I was still determined that I could make it and my racing in Belgium had only confirmed to me that I had all that was necessary to win and beat anyone.

It seemed no time at all before I was back in Mr. Cowhig's office for I had been invited to ride with a British team on the indoor track in East Berlin. It was about a ten day trip altogether and I asked for my fortnight's summer holiday. Mr. Cowhig said O.K., although he had, I am sure, some reservations about me rushing off again so soon after I had supposedly settled down to work again.

I had a great time in East Germany and thoroughly enjoyed myself. The track was a very hard one for it had very steep bankings—56 degrees—and I had quite a num-

ber of spills. One of them was in a sprint match against the
East German sprint champion and happened when we were
going slow on the top of the banking. I was in front and
trying to get him to take over the lead when I just went too
slowly for the bike to stay upright. Whoosh! down I slid,
and the German, who was now almost alongside me, turned
his machine straight down in an effort to prevent a collision.
He could not pull out on the steep slope and rode off the
track, breaking his collarbone in the process. A rather unusual way of getting rid of the opposition!

The East Germans were pleased with my riding and asked
me if I would stay and ride a six-hour madison with a German partner the following week. I jumped at the chance
for I knew that the experience of riding such a race on an
indoor track would be of good use to me. I naturally accepted and so extended my stay while the other Englishmen
returned home.

It was terrific and my partner and I were well in with a
chance of victory until, with only twenty minutes left, I
crashed again. Going round the banking I was 'chopped' by
another rider whose rear wheel nut took my front wheel
straight out. Bang! Down I went and on to a stretcher, finishing up in the track infirmary. It was nothing serious and I
came home feeling great, despite my numerous cuts and
bruises.

I knew now that the Continent was for me and that I
stood a good chance of success in the professional class, but
I would have to go and fight my way into it. I suppose the
idea had been buzzing around in my head for a long time,
maybe right from the day I first rode a bike. I just knew that
I was capable of beating anyone and, just like when I left
my club at Harworth to improve my standards, I had to go
and prove myself. This time, of course, things were different
and much, much bigger than those early days.

As soon as I got home I wrote away to the Murphy brothers in France. They were two young riders I had met at Manchester and on the Isle of Man, and both spoke a little English. I asked Robert and Yvon when would be the best time to come over, and if I could stay with them. They were good lads and an answer came back by return of post that the season started in April and they looked forward to seeing me.

This was just after Easter, so I planned to ride the British tracks over the holiday and then go out the following Tuesday. It was a decision that was to affect my whole future.

# 7

# Into the Unknown

As I mentioned, I was very fit and really 'flying' when I came back from East Germany so I was able to clean up on the tracks during the Easter holiday. I went to the Good Friday Meeting at Herne Hill and rode behind the big motors specially brought over from Germany. The East German visitors were impressed with my riding and asked if I would like to go out there to train. They said that I could win the 'demi-fonde' for amateurs in the next World Championship, and they would be happy to look after me.

It was my first attempt at riding these events where you can get up some tremendous speeds behind the big, specially built motor cycles. I had had a go in training when I was in East Berlin and was sure I could ride well. It was a fabulous offer and my first impulse was to get off to the Continent in a different manner from the one I had planned.

What an offer though! They would really have looked after me there and I would, despite being an amateur, have been virtually professional, for they would have provided all my accommodation, food and pocket money plus, of course, the prizes I would pick up at events. Then, at the end of it there was a possible world title. Heck! Possible? I know I would have won it!

At the same time there was also an offer for me to join the Elswick Hopper independent team in England. They were a good squad and managed by Benny Foster, who had become more than a manager to me, for he had many times given me wise counsel. He was there at Herne Hill so I took my dilemma to him to find out his views on it.

We had a long talk, going over all the ground, and he told me that I would ruin my chances of bigger things if I threw everything else up and went behind the motors. As far as England was concerned, well, I knew that my capabilities would not be extended and he said that I would severely limit my horizons by staying here. I really knew all this all the time, but just needed that confirmation from somebody else. Benny gave me that and the final bit of confidence I needed.

Easter Saturday saw me right in form at Cardiff, where I won everything that I rode. A rest on the following day and then I was at it again at Fallowfield. There was an international omnium where I won every event in the series except the 'devil', in which I was disqualified for chopping up Norman Shiel!

It was quite a laugh—for me, anyway! We were the only two left, the others having been eliminated, and were rounding the final bend for the sprint finish. I was high up the banking and he came through on the inside. I took a flier off the bank as he came round the bend and suddenly moved across him as he entered the straight. There was nothing poor Norman could do but run off the track, which he did, holding up his hand in protest. This was upheld and while we had a good laugh about it later, I am sure he was not too pleased at the time!

We had known each other for a long time and had raced together in many countries, and he was a great companion, except when talking about bike riding. Here he was always

the master tactician and a man who would carefully prepare himself for the big races. He would never 'let on' to
me about his theories because, I think, good racing man that
he was, he regarded me as his natural enemy so gave away
none of his secrets. Nevertheless he was a great rider and
Britain could always do with a few more like him.

I rode the final race of the day—the International 10-
mile event—and won that too, thus completing a very successful holiday of racing. On the way back home that night
I realised that I would be leaving England the next day and
found a bit of the old 'butterflies' inside me. I had lost a lot
of my nervousness now. I suppose I had grown up more, and
experience had helped too, but I was a bit apprehensive of
what awaited me on the other side.

Having worked hard since my return from Belgium, I had
managed to save £100 and this was the fortune I took out of
the bank to see me on the road to success abroad. A friend
of mine, Bill Womack, had taken my two bikes, one road,
one track, down to Doncaster Station for me and so I did
not have too much to carry when I left home. Too much!
All my worldly possessions were contained in two suitcases
and a haversack on my back, and I was also clutching a pair
of wheels.

I do not think I had told anyone about my plans, and
hardly had time to say a proper 'Goodbye' to my mother.
Out of the front door and down the path, out through the
gate and off up the road to the bus-stop I went. Here was the
spirit of great adventure, and when I thought soberly about
it for a moment, I knew it would be the final and supreme
test. No pause, no looking back, no 'hammy' acting scenes
as I left the street behind. The same street that I had ridden
round as a boy of twelve and had first been bitten by the
cycling bug. No cares and no regrets. Funny, isn't it? I soon
thought about it all when I was in France and things were

getting me down, but that's the way of life. One never seems to miss things until they are not there any more.

As I got on the bus my father stepped off. There were only a few moments to break the news that I was leaving for France. 'Oh, aye!' he said, with remarkable calmness, 'good luck then, lad.' My thanks were shouted back from the platform of the bus as it moved off, and I watched him disappear down the road. I remember thinking 'he doesn't care about me, and he'll expect me home again soon.' How wrong can you get? I heard a long time afterwards that the old man had gone straight into the 'local' and ordered a pint. He said to the landlord: 'Eh! bloody 'ell, Bill, my lad's got to go to France for his racing.' He picked up the glass, looked at it and put it down again. Tears came into his eyes and he said: 'It's a bogger!' Once more he picked up the pint, once more he looked at it, and then, without another word, replaced it on the counter, not having touched a drop, and walked out.

I arrived in France without any difficulty and, because of my lack of French, fell foul of a taxi-driver who charged me forty francs for a short journey between railway stations! More trouble was to come when I arrived at St. Brieuc in Brittany where the Murphys lived. I got into the local station at about half past five in the morning and then tried to find the house.

I kept asking people for 'Murphy, Butchers, please' and was directed all over the place. They were, or Mr. Murphy senior was, a butcher, and so I thought they would be easy to find. Not a bit of it. I kept pushing my two bikes with my two suitcases and my haversack strapped on my back all over the town. They had me going in all directions, and I must have walked miles and miles before I eventually located them. By then it was nearly half past one and I felt a proper nit, I can tell you.

The Murphy family soon had me feeling at home despite not really understanding what they were saying to me. Although Robert, whom I always called 'Bert', and his brother Yvon spoke a smattering of English, I often wonder how on earth we managed to converse at all, as my own grasp of their language was practically non-existent. Their name, as you will have no doubt realised, was not typically French and Monsieur Murphy told me that his grandparents were Irish. He explained to me that his great-grandfather was an Irish priest!

How he managed it I shall never know but his efforts, for he spoke no English at all, are engraved upon my memory for ever. It really must have been the all-time mammoth miming act and you can just imagine the arm-waving, pointing at pictures and gesticulations that went on between the two of us.

I had not felt excited or elated at all during my journey across, perhaps because I was travelling alone, but when I reached the Murphy house I was ready to talk for hours. Of course this was impossible and began to get me down straight away. I suppose I am a naturally talkative chap and the inability to converse with anybody, even just remarking about the weather or things like that, made me very glum.

Yet I was quickly able to adapt myself to the ways of this French cycling family and found the food good and wholesome. After four days I managed to enter my first event, a local 'criterium' or 'round the houses' race. I decided to try for the primes and not do anything drastic. This word is really only known to the cycling fraternity in general, and being French, is pronounced 'preem'. It means a subsidiary prize within the race and can take the form of a hill climb award or a lap prize.

In these circuit races there are usually prizes on every lap and I won several of these before I punctured and had to retire. In a few days I was racing again in the criteriums and in a number of these there were a lot of professionals, men who had ridden the big events, even the Tour de France, and I was curious to find out how I would fare against them.

It was not long before I was out-sprinting them for lap primes and I realised they were not so good as I had originally thought, which bucked me up a great deal and encouraged me to try hard and win. The language problem presented difficulties when racing because I had to find a rider who could tell me where the primes were so that I knew where to sprint, and I sometimes had trouble in finding out when the last lap was on!

Difficulties also began to come my way from various authorities. First, I had a rather curt letter from the British Cycling Federation, who warned me about riding against professionals with an amateur licence. I thought this was a bit much for I had applied to them for an independent licence way back in March before I left for France, and it still had not come through. Instead they sent me this letter and even complained about my riding there without asking their permission! It was true that a rider had to get their consent to ride abroad, but I did not think they would mind me going.

Another thing which had cropped up was that my call-up papers had arrived at home just after I had left. Lucky me! National Service was still on in England and I had been deferred when I was eighteen because I was sitting for my various exams to become a draughtsman. I had, in fact, been approached by the R.A.F. for they were very keen to have good sportsmen and obviously put me into that category with my cycling successes.

I had been quite happy about joining and had, in fact, had my medical in the summer of 1958 when, incidentally,

they found I am slightly colour-blind. It was not very serious
and was discovered only when I had to sort out a lot of col-
ours and could not distinguish between blue and purple.
It has never bothered me in ordinary life and I can always
pick out the necessary jersey when I must!

In all the excitement of going to the World Championship and then off to Switzerland and Belgium and back to
Germany, plus my coming to France, I had forgotten all
about it. Anyway, I was safe now, I thought, and my mother
sent the papers back, telling them I was now in France.
That would be the end of that I imagined, but I had not
heard the last of it, as I was to find out.

I won my next four events and as a result found myself
very much in the public eye. I was news, and the publicity
that I had managed to attract got me my first sponsor. This
was one of many local wine-making firms, which had about
fifty riders under its 'marque'. I had, at last, obtained my
independent licence and was out of trouble in the official
sense and well into the swing of things.

My sudden benefactor, the wine man, was a shrewd sort
of chap because I did not realise that when he put me into
certain events he may have been under-paying me! It could
not have been very much in those days but it goes to show
what can happen when you are not only green but also,
because of language difficulties, unable to speak up for yourself!

I did not find out about this for many years and would
probably never have done so except for a remark made
to me by a race promoter soon after I had won the
World title. He had asked me to ride an event for which he
promised to pay me good money. He said to me when he
paid me, 'You are a bit more expensive than you were in
1959, Monsieur Simpson!' I just smiled and agreed with
him. It did not dawn on me at first that I had been 'done' all

those years back and the realisation of it gave me a good laugh. After all, it was a long time ago and anyway I had a lot to thank my wine boss for and so I just tucked the incident away in the experience folder.

My beginnings in France had been most successful from a racing point of view, but I was getting more and more lonely as the days wore on. Lack of company, in terms of conversation, began to tell and I really longed to have a good old chat with someone. I had been there for about two weeks, and, apart from the odd few words with the Murphy brothers, I might just as well have been dumb. Then came a surprise which made all the difference.

# 8

# More Milestones

ONE day I returned to my digs to find the Murphys grinning all over their faces. I was told, with much sign language and hand-waving, that an English girl was staying in the same street with a French family and acting as an 'au pair'. They wrote down the number of the house and off I went, feeling quite elated. For the first time since I had arrived I felt like the real me. My spirits soared as I realised that not only was I going to be able to speak properly to someone, but that I was also going to meet a girl.

I had had a few girl friends in England, but nothing very serious and, because of my training schedules and early bed-times, did not have much time for courting, but I was a normal lad whose head turned at the sight of the female figures, so I trotted off down the street, happily filled with thoughts of gorgeous blondes.

I suppose I would not have cared what colour hair she had for the main thought was that I would, at long last, have someone to talk to and, perhaps, learn some French. I marched up to the house and, climbing the few steps, rang the bell. Within a few seconds I froze with horror. What, I asked myself, will happen if she does not answer the door? Here am I, unable to speak more than a little of the language, ringing some Frenchman's doorbell and, if the owner comes out I will be totally incapable of making him understand why I am here. I do not know how long I actually stood on the doorstep as I thought about it, not long I am sure, and since no-one had opened the door, I decided to depart and quickly!

I could not have been there for more than ten seconds and shot off down the street trying to look as unconcerned as possible, and as though I had never been near the door-bell at all. I felt rather like a schoolboy who did that sort of thing as a joke and walked along, thrusting my hands in my pockets and whistling loudly. I was sure the eyes of the whole street were on me, but there were no shouts or cries of anger and I retreated into my own lodgings without look-ing back or arousing suspicion.

I explained to the Murphys, with the usual laborious sign language, that nobody was at home, to justify my returning so soon, and my depression came back even more firmly than before. A few days later with the gloom well settled upon me, I was sitting in the garden reading when a girl came up to the front entrance and asked: *'C'est ici ou le jeune Anglais habite?'* Well, I had been to a certain degree, the centre of attraction in the area, partly because I was English and had won a few races. Now and then people popped in and I was like one of those freaks in the circus sideshows, and my mood was not one which welcomed being looked over by the neighbourhood.

I didn't understand what she said and just growled: 'Bogger off! Why can't people leave me alone?' Imagine my surprise and embarrassment when she replied: 'Oh, it's you, is it? I wondered if you'd be in.' Yes, you guessed it. It was the English girl from down the street and she had heard about the 'English boy' staying nearby and, like me, wanted very much to have a good old natter.

It was like Heaven being able to talk again, and she en-joyed it too. We were soon chattering away for all we were

worth and I was quite staggered to find that she was a Yorkshire lass and, even more of a coincidence, lived not far from
my own home at Harworth. Her name was Helen Sherburn
and, naturally, we got on like a house on fire and I became a
much happier man.

We used to visit each other's digs and go walking together,
always finding plenty to talk about. Because of racing I was
often away in different areas and so we did not see too much
of each other. I remember once I had persuaded her to come
out to see me race at a town about four kilometres away from
St. Brieuc. She had to arrange the Sunday off specially, as
she usually took the children out for a walk. On this particular Sunday she set out on foot to see the event. What
happened I do not know because she never saw the race
and I got a telling-off the next time we met as she had practically walked her feet off going there and back!

I was doing quite well now and getting used to the racing
and, at the end of April, began to take some French lessons.
Helen spoke good French and she helped too, but I took
proper tuition from an Englishman in the town, Professor
Batman. He was marvellous and had quite a pronunciation
job on his hands because of my north country accent. He
would spend whole lessons just getting me to practise certain
sounds in front of a mirror to make sure that my mouth
made the correct shape. I had quite a few laughs with Helen
over this and pulled all sorts of weird faces in front of her,
explaining that this or that contorted face was most essential for the learner!

Learning was a slow process though, especially as I was
always popping off to various places in Brittany to race.
Many people in the area were now my 'supporters' and frequently I would get one or more talking away to me before
the start of the race, giving all sorts of advice and telling
me what to do. It was funny really because I would stand

there, apparently taking it all in, saying 'Oui, oui', and
hardly understanding a word. I am sure they got exasperated
when they saw their advice being ignored, but I could not
do anything about it, except keep on with my French lessons.

I rode in my first stage race in May, the 'Essor Breton',
a four-day race for riders under 25 which took in the Brittany peninsula. As usual the supporters were there with their
customary well-intended comments and I well remember
being approached at the start of the third stage by an
elderly Frenchman. He was an 'Onion Johnnie' who had
travelled in England, selling his wares to housewives in
Bradford and around the West Riding of Yorkshire. His
broken English was almost as difficult to understand as his
French, but he wanted me to attack that day and told me
when and where to do it. He was a nice old chap and had
been in Doncaster and was very proud of his British associa-
tions.

Well, I could not honestly remember the name of the
town that he told me and so did not make a break at all that
day, and, much to my surprise, there he was at the finish and
he gave me quite a telling-off for not having done a good
ride! Next morning there he was again, his red, friendly
face shining out from under his blue beret and surrounded
by an aroma of garlic and red wine. In his quaint broken
English he told me I must break away at Fau and that he
would be there at the roadside with a flag which, incidentally, turned out to be a Union Jack! When I saw the flag
I must make my effort.

What could I do but try? Sure enough, as we rode
through the town, there he was, waving the flag at the roadside, his red face redder than ever with the excitement. I
attacked at the bottom of a small hill as we left the town,
and got free with another rider. For ten kilometres I stayed
at the front and then moved over and motioned the other

man to come through. What he said I mistook for a swear-word, but found out afterwards that he, in fact, gasped 'Too fast, I can't do it!' Anyhow, I went off up the road, leaving him behind and won the stage quite easily.

It had been a good race for me for I had ended with a stage victory and second place overall, being only two seconds behind the winner. This got me a lot more publicity and I received an offer to join the Margnat/Rochet professional team. I turned it down mainly because I had now lost some of my impulsiveness (thank goodness!) and wanted to see what would happen after I had had a little more experience of the bigger races. I did not have to wait long. Shortly after the finish of the 'Essor Breton' I received a letter from the St. Rapha/V.C.12, the Club behind the St. Raphael-Geminiani professional team. They asked me if I would like to ride in their team in the Route de France, an eight stage race, again for riders under twenty-five years old. This was a great honour and they must have gone to some trouble to get me in. The event is open only to French national teams. There are usually three of them and they are listed 'A', 'B' and 'C', plus regional teams from all over the country. I could not ride in the West team, but, as the only foreigner, I was able to get into the Rápha/V.C.12 squad. Naturally I accepted, thinking it would be a race like the previous one, with fairly easy stages.

I got quite a shock when I found that the first stage was 196 kilometres! This was covered in the pouring rain at an average speed of over 27 m.p.h., and I was sitting almost terrified in the bunch all the way! What I did not want to happen, above all else, was that I should not be there at the finish, and so I watched how I went very carefully indeed.

I had never ridden such a long distance in a road race before, but felt quite all right after that first day. On the second day we moved into the mountains for the next five days, and I got my first taste of real mountain climbing. Before we started I was filled with trepidation about how I would fare on the big climbs and tried to get some advice from the team mechanic. My French was still very bad and he had a difficult task trying to explain to me what to do. 'Keep within your capabilities. Have something in hand' was what he tried to tell me but I just could not get it. Then he made a slow pedalling motion with his hands, saying 'Touriste, touriste', and I got it. He wanted me to ride the 'cols' like a tourist, nice and easy, and so I did. I was with a small breakaway when we reached the foot of the giant Tourmalet climb, known to all followers of the Tour de France. I put in my smallest gear and began to climb. I found it quite easy as I rode the near fifteen miles to the summit, which takes you 9,000 feet up and, at the top, passed over comfortably, not even sweating, but ten minutes down on the last rider! That was my first lesson how to climb cols and I had plenty more in the next five days when I found out an awful lot about climbing and descending, and fell several times, which taught me to be more careful.

It was awe-inspiring at first going up the Toumalet, for great banks of snow were piled high on either side of the road for many miles. I had never seen anything quite like it before and felt very small and insignificant. Still, I was learning fast although I still had the dread inside me that I would not finish, a disgrace which I could not face.

My French got me into trouble when we stayed at Pau at the end of a stage during the mountains sections, for I was told something wrong by the other riders. I wanted to know how to enquire where the toilet was and, not realising at all that my leg was being pulled, was told to say '*Avez-vous un chiotte, s'il vous plait?*' This seemed quite easy and so I walked into our hotel for the night and said this to the

lady at the reception desk. I should have known something
was wrong for a number of grinning riders had followed me
in and were standing around, well within earshot.

The woman looked so shocked by my request that I
knew I had said something wrong and felt positively awful
when she brought her husband out to me! Everything was
explained away quite quickly and fortunately they accepted
my profuse apologies! My enquiry turned out to be basically
correct, and basic is the right word! It was hardly the thing
to say to a lady, particularly a strange one, for the word is
rather a vulgar description of a toilet. One which, I may
add, would certainly not be approved in England!

The race progressed and I went through my ordeal in the
mountains quite well and was still in the race as we started
the final stage. The news of my clanger at the hotel had gone
round and everyone had a good laugh at my expense. The
journalists travelling with us had thought it a capital joke
and I think this helped me with them for they always 'interviewed' me after stages in the hope that some 'pearls of wisdom' would come from my lips! Certainly it put me on good
terms with all of them, which was very useful.

We had been riding for some time on that last day when
I suddenly saw a road sign which said '76 kms. Hossneger'.
I knew that was the finish and quickly calculated the kilometres into miles. Joyfully I realised that there were only
about 47 miles to the finish and I knew I would finish the
race. After living with my heart in my mouth for the previous seven days it was a great relief and I suppose I suffered
from a complaint which affects many British riders—the
fear of extending oneself too far and too early.

I was so elated that I put my head down and went! Only
one man followed me up the road and we got a small lead
of about 100 yards. After about 15 miles we were no further
ahead and he said it was no good and dropped back to the

bunch. I had the bit between my teeth and kept going. Still the gap remained the same and with 400 yards to the line they caught up with me. Everyone was going now, eyeballs hanging out, and I think they had all shot their bolts trying to get up to me. Anyway, I held on and nobody got past me. I had won my first big stage race victory!

I was like a man in a dream for a time, and when everyone went to Paris my great moment came when I met the great Monsieur Louviot, the Directeur Sportif of the St. Raphael-Geminiani team. He said he was very impressed by my riding and gave me a St. Raphael jersey and two tubular tyres. He asked me if I would ride for him in the Tour of the West and urged me to make sure I was properly prepared and did not lose too many races in the next two months. I was absolutely delighted and, of course, said 'Yes'.

Before returning to St. Brieuc I stayed in Paris where my lack of French once more got me into an embarrassing situation. It was in a restaurant where I had a most enjoyable meal. It had not been difficult to explain what I wanted, but the real trouble began when I had to ask for the bill. I had no idea what to say and thought that the waitress would bring it along without my having to ask. I sat there for ages and she eventually came over and asked '*L'addition, Monsieur?*' Thinking she was asking me if I wanted more to eat, I shook my head and said '*non!*' I had no idea she was asking me if I wanted the bill, and sat there miserably wondering when it would arrive.

She came up to me a number of times with the same query, and each time she got the same shake of the head and the same glum '*Non!*' I think about two hours passed in this manner before the owner himself joined in and then everything was sorted out.

My ride in the Route de France had spread far and

wide through France, via the national newspapers, and the
Murphys honoured me by arriving at St. Brieuc station to
meet me, in the family car. M. Murphy gave me the traditional kiss on both cheeks and I was treated very much
like a minor conquering hero.

# 9

# The World of Professionals

THE time passed quickly. May went into June and then July. I saw Helen Sherburn again quite a lot while I was in St. Brieuc and we enjoyed many a good old chat in English, although my French was improving by leaps and bounds. She was to leave France soon and spend a month at home in England before going out to a family in Stuttgart there to learn German, which, incidentally, she spoke quite well—by my standards, anyway!

I had my first taste of the really big-time professionals at a track meeting at Landerneau, where I was partnered by Hubert Ferrer, the then French Army champion. He was staying with me at the Murphy home and was quite a good rider. Between us we slaughtered the 'pros' and they became very annoyed with us.

I well remember Hassenforder, better known to the crowds as 'The Clown' but to the riders as 'The Bandit'. He got rather upset with me for I beat him in a sprint, a points race and an elimination series. Ferrer also did well and we were cock-a-hoop with ourselves. There were quite a few good men there and all of them had finished the Tour de France only the day before.

Jean Stablinski, who later became World Road Champion, Jean Grazcyk, François Mahé and a number of others were also annoyed when we beat them in a number of

races including a Madison. I had reason to understand why
they were so angry with us when I rode the Tour the following year, and now appreciate how they must have felt!
Had I been more used to the 'pro' game I would never have
treated them so cockily for they are good riders, but I was
eventually forgiven for my hot-headedness.

It was not long before the great day arrived, and I started
the Tour of the West with the Rapha team. I was just one of
only a few independents riding and all the big names, with
the exception of Rik Van Looy and Jacques Anquetil, were
there. I was no longer worried about the distances and
was confident that I could ride well among such exalted
riders and was more or less used to 'pro' racing.

On the first of the eight days' racing, I got into a breakaway group and finished well up in the placings. We were a
good team and at the end of the next day we had the
leader's jersey in our squad. This was gained by Pierre Everaert and we all worked hard to protect him. For three days
we kept the lead and then, on the following day, a break
developed at the front which gained a lead of about four
minutes. This time-lag meant that Everaert had lost his
overall lead, and also worrying was the fact that we had no
one from the team up in front. I tried to take Everaert up
but he did not stay with me and soon after breaking free I
had four men latched on to my wheel. They refused to work,
knowing that they had members of their own teams in the
forward group. So I had to tow them along.

I caught the leading group only about a kilometre from
the line and immediately launched myself into a sprint. I
was clear and crossed the line just about three lengths ahead
of the next rider, to take over the race leadership! What a
moment that was! I was so excited that I could hardly speak
for my French, although improving, was not equal to this!

On the following day I won the time trial stage and increased my overall lead to almost three minutes. Then we had to cover the longest stage of the Tour, about 150 miles from Brest to St. Brieuc—my home town, as it were. I was not too worried about winning the stage there, although I knew the townsfolk would be rooting for me. As things turned out it was a bad day for me. Quite early, a break got going and nobody bothered to chase but soon after the halfway mark had gone, something had to be done. The other members of the team told me not to worry for they would protect me and anyway, one of our riders, Morvan, was with the break and might help to slow things down. Eventually the group were about six minutes in advance of us and the pace of the bunch started to rise. Then, just as we were beginning to pull them back, I punctured. Jean Claude Lefevre immediately gave me his machine, but it was too big for me and I could not get going properly. I finished with the main field, but had lost the lead.

A lot of people were vexed when they heard that our rider, Morvan, had been working very hard in the break-away and although he was dropped just before the finish, he had enough time in hand to take over the jersey from me. It was a great disappointment, for I had hoped the attitude of the team would have been different towards me, but I learned to understand that it was hard for a young rider to stake his claim so early in the professional world. At the same time I also realised that not one of them in that race could beat me individually when I was going well and could do so only when resorting to team riding.

I was comforted by this discovery and gained a lot of confidence which was certainly needed for the World Championship a fortnight or so later.

The French papers set up quite a hullabaloo over Morvan winning instead of me, and I probably received more publicity than the winner himself, for they said he stole my race.

René De Latour, a well-known French journalist, carried the headline over the race story, 'The Tour he should never have lost' so I suppose I did very well out of it. Certainly I did so financially considering my small beginnings, for Rapha came forward with a contract for me. I had ridden the event without being paid but now they offered me 400NF.—about £28 10s. 0d. per month. In addition, Louviot, the Directeur Sportif, came up and said he would raise this by another 100 francs (about £7 10s.) per month to compensate me for the loss of the race. This was very generous of him and I signed on the dotted line.

After a short rest I was soon on my way to Amsterdam for the World Cycling Championships, where the track events were to be my first goal as a professional. I was in very good form, and on arrival at my hotel found a letter waiting for me. It was from the British Federation who, at long last, had sent my professional licence. I had ridden with the 'pros' for long enough now not to feel elated about getting the licence I had wanted for a very long time, and since I had at last got a sponsor who was actually paying me money, it did not affect my emotions much. I had thought they might have sent me a note with it saying 'good luck' or something, but I suppose there was no news at all in England about my successes.

I went for the World Professional Pursuit title, honestly believing I would win, as I just could not accept the fact that anyone was better, specially after my good rides over the past few months! But I was in for a bitter disappointment. Despite the fact that I qualified with the third fastest time, I was put out in the quarter-finals. My world went to pieces and I can hardly remember a thing about the occasion. How many times before had I had this happen to me? No matter how many I still had not become used to picking up my shattered ego and found it as hard to take as ever.

Tommy Godwin, the British team manager, was there and I sometimes think that if it had not been for him I would really have packed up for good. Crestfallen is hardly the word to describe me as I wheeled by bike off the track and down the tunnel towards the changing rooms. Tommy came down with me and as we walked along he put his arm round my shoulder to comfort me. It was the last straw and I broke down and wept like a child, my bike falling to the ground unnoticed. He was wonderful, for I am sure he wanted to cry too, but knew that he must talk some sense into me. Gradually he talked me round and made things seem brighter and I began to concentrate on all the things that I had read in the letters from George Berger, and the advice from Cyril Cartwright. Tommy was chatting to me in much the same way and he helped to put some of my spirit back, so I decided to ride in the road race after all.

The event took place on the motor racing circuit at Zandewoort and covered a total distance of some 180 miles. This was the longest race I had so far entered, but having recovered from my downfall in the pursuit, I had my old confidence back. As we went to the start I felt quite ready to beat all of them and found a lot of reassurance in seeing around me many riders I had raced against in the Tour of the West.

The course covered about 20 laps and almost right from the start a small group of ten riders broke clear. Soon they held a lead of about one and a half minutes and for a time no one bothered to get up to them. After a few laps several riders made attempts to reach them but they all failed and I eventually decided to go after them. I went away with Fischerkeller of Germany and, within the space of a lap, we were on.

At the halfway mark, and holding a lead of two minutes,

our group was down to eight men. The others were bene-
fiting from my inexperience now, for while they were not
exactly sitting on me, they would only do half the amount of
work at the front. My impulsiveness and 'I'll show 'em' attitude made me keep going, and anyway, I really was feeling
good.

I knew only two men in the party, Geldermans and another Dutchman, the former having been in the Rapha
Team in the Tour of the West. What I did not know was
that the fair-haired man in the French national jersey was
André Darrigade, a renowned sprinter and winner of many
stages in the Tour de France. Another thing I did not know
was that Darrigade had combined with the two Dutchmen
to ensure that I did not win. I had no idea of this at the time
and only found out later when they got into trouble with the
Dutch Federation. It was certainly pleasant to learn that
they feared me as much as that!

We got down to the last three laps and I knew I must
try to get clear again on my own if I was to have a good
chance of victory. Several times I tried to break and each
time, after getting clear, was pulled back by the others. A
strong north wind was blowing across from the sea now and
made lone rides very difficult, but there was nothing I could
do now except wait for the sprint.

Not knowing the ability of the others I selected the Belgian, Foré, as the man who could possibly lead me out in
the final sprint, but I chose the wrong man. I do not think
I would have made it, even if he had been better, for I
was very tired after all the work I had done. He was not by
any means fast, but even so, when the moment came, my
legs would not go and I could not even get round him, so
had to be content with fourth place watching Darrigade take
it.

He was very good, actually, for he praised my efforts in

the interviews with the Press, a big-hearted thing to do. He said that I had ridden magnificently and was sure it was because of my strong riding that the group did not get caught. His kindness in saying this helped me a lot, for the papers all carried the comments and I obtained a number of good contracts to ride in events immediately afterwards.

I travelled considerably around Europe after this and took part in the Tour of Lombardy and the Trophy Barrachi for the first time in Italy. In the latter event, I rode against my old idol, Fausto Coppi, and had quite a thrill out of riding in the same event as the 'Campionissimo'. I finished fourth and thus ended the season on a fairly high note. I had been in most of the later events with another Rapha rider, the Frenchman Gerard Saint, who was both a good 'bikie' and a good companion, but tragically, he was killed in a road accident about six months later.

I returned home reasonably triumphant after my long racing spell to find an awful lot of people who wanted to talk about my riding and, for the first time in my life, I gave cycling a rest for a time, to enjoy a holiday.

Out and about with various friends I naturally looked at the girls again, for I had virtually forgotten their existence during my racing. My thoughts turned to Helen Sherburn, now in Germany, and as she had given me her address before she left France, I wrote to her.

I suppose I was her boy-friend in a way, but we were not really very close in St. Brieuc and I cannot ever remember even holding her hand or kissing her, and when I wrote to her I always signed myself 'Yours sincerely' for I was not a very forward lad when it came to romance and I was not all that interested in her, or so I thought then. It's strange how one discovers that a girl means a lot. It happened this way.

In the next few weeks I wrote to Helen a number of times

and she replied. Then, when talking to some of the lads one night, I said casually, 'I met a lovely girl in France. She was English too', and as soon as I had said it I knew I was in love with her and there was nobody else for me.

# 10

# The Story of the Call-up

THERE was not very much I could do about Miss Sherburn
all those miles away, but I sent her a small gold chain for
Christmas. I think it took her by surprise for she had not
bought me a present. About this time, I met her parents who,
of course, lived not very far from Doncaster, and I also
went round to see someone else who lived locally—Brian
Robinson.

He had been on the Continent for a few years and was,
as you probably recall, one of my 'heroes' when I was younger. Already he was an old hand at the Tour de France and
the pro game in general, and since we were to be in the same
team together, we would obviously be seeing quite a bit of
the racing with each other. He was to be a good friend and
adviser to me, especially during the coming year, for what he
lacked in the legs he made up for in the head!

When I came home I must have upset somebody who was
either jealous of my 28 wins in my first full season abroad, or
just did not like me. Whatever the reason, the word was passed along to the authorities that I was back home and was
not it about time I was called up? Immediately after Christmas a letter arrived summoning me to another medical.
That was the first intimation I had had that they were gun-
ning for me.

It seemed illogical, for I have never dodged my call-up, and now that I had become established as a professional abroad, everything was likely to be wrecked. I felt rather cross about it but there was nothing I could do, and so in the first few days of January, 1960, I reported to Sheffield for a second medical.

I was passed fit and then called into an office—I think it was that of the Enlisting Officer. I was asked to sit down and the Officer pulled out a file marked 'Simpson'. 'Ah! You're one of those special cases, are you?' he said, and asked me a few questions about what I had been doing. I answered them and he said: 'Well, we'll soon have you in, young feller. When are you supposed to be going back to France?' I told him it was the next day. This was perfectly true for I had arranged to travel out to the St. Raphael training camp at Norbonne in the south of France with Robinson. He did not seem to like that very much and asked for my address. '15 Rue de Rennes, St. Brieuc, Cote du Nord,' I replied quite truthfully. 'No, no,' he said, 'your proper address in England.' I told him that the French address was correct for I was only staying with my parents in England. Anyway he wanted that address and I gave it to him and that was that.

I left for France, as arranged, with 'Robbo', the next day, and soon after I reached the training camp I had a letter from my mother telling me that my call-up papers had arrived the day after I left! She had returned them once more and again I thought that was an end to the matter. But I was wrong.

The affair had received some publicity in the Press, both at home and abroad, and I remember thinking that it was just like the British papers to stir things without ever really giving my racing successes a good 'plug'. The French papers regarded it all as a huge joke, but Helen told me that in

Germany they reported that I was the man 'who would not fight for his Queen'.

Whatever the ifs and buts of the affair, I was certainly not going to let it interfere with my chosen career after all the hard work I had done. I arrived at the training camp, which was under the direction of M. Louviot, and in all the training, discussions and talks he made me realise just how right had been my early tutors Berger, Cartwright and Foster. I did not have very much to learn on the actual training side, but on racing tactics I needed the advice. I shared a room with a Frenchman, Nicholas Baron, who was probably the most immaculate bike rider I have ever met. He was always beautifully dressed, generally wearing light suits, and was the only man I know who could wear a white raincoat for a month and not get it dirty! In addition, he was a very good rider and rode the Tour de France many times, nearly always gaining the 'Prix d'Elegance' awarded to the smartest rider in the race. He would ride in any event and still look clean and polished after it, while others would come in covered in mud and filthy dirty. His career had been sadly interrupted the previous year by a car accident and he was now trying hard to get back on form.

Another inmate at the training camp was Roger Hassenforder, the 'Clown' or the 'Bandit'—he was well-known by either nickname. He was a very amusing man and usually had us all in fits of laughter with his many and varied antics and tricks. The stories of him are legion and legend throughout the cycling world, and he was dearly loved by the public everywhere.

He taught me the importance of being able to make people laugh, for as a professional it was part and parcel of the job. He had been in a very bad accident as a young boy and it was remarkable that he walked, let alone rode a bike. Apparently, just after the war he had collected a variety of

old shells and other types of ammunition which he put
in a hole in a field, together with a few cans of petrol. It was
his intention to let off the 'Hassenforder atom bomb' and
laid a trail of gunpowder back from the arsenal and lit it.
He had built himself a trench but had not reached it
when everything blew up and he was caught by the
blast.

He was taken to Switzerland to hospital as there was nowhere in France then which could have taken proper care
of the terrible burns he had sustained on his legs and back.
There are many stories of how he became a bike rider and
he, himself, says that he had the misfortune to kill someone
once and was found guilty of manslaughter so, because he
had to pay an enormous fine, he turned to riding a bike to
earn the money! This was another of his jokes, of course!

Sometimes in races which passed through small towns and
villages he would ride close to the pavement and snatch the
hat from some unsuspecting spectator's head. He tried this
once on an old lady all dressed up in her best clothes and it
was not until he had grabbed it that he found it was tied
under her chin!

Probably he was never ticked off so emphatically or so
fast in all his days!

On another occasion he was invited to open a new track
in a town and, with other riders, to take part in the in-
augural meeting which followed. The Mayor produced a
pair of large ceremonial scissors for him to cut the tape across
the track and Hassenforder leaned forward, and before cutting the tape, snipped off the major portion of the Mayor's
tie and solemnly handed it to that very surprised dig-
nitary!

I remember another occasion when he was invited to a
banquet arranged by the U.C.I. (International Cycling
Union) in Paris, together with the French national team.

Everyone sat through the meal waiting for Hassenforder to
do something funny or outrageous, but nothing happened.
At the end of it all they retired to an antechamber for coffee
etc., and as Hassenforder walked into the crowded room, he
pulled up his shirt and released three pigeons. It was absolute pandemonium in there for a time, as the three frightened birds flew in all directions, knocking down great clouds
of dust from the chandeliers. The occupants were scurrying
about trying to dodge out of the way of the dust, and, at
the same time, attempting to keep their suits from becoming
'spotted' by the panic-stricken pigeons! That was Hassenforder, and although I have grown to enjoy a bit of clowning
for a crowd, I do not think I will ever match up to the things
he did.

No sooner were we out of the training camp than it was
time for racing again and early March saw me in one of the
longest road classics, Milan–San Remo. That year it was
made a little harder by the inclusion of the sharp climb of the
Poggio Hill just before entering San Remo and at the end
of the ride. René De Latour had said that I could win this
race, and after listening to him I launched myself into the
attack on the very first climb. At the summit I was a minute
clear and rode away onto level road once more, two minutes
in advance of the bunch. But I was beaten because,
although my French had improved, I had misunderstood
what had been said and thought there were only 70 kilometres to the finish when, in fact, there were one hundred
and ten!

I rode alone for over 40 miles and was caught on the
Poggio climb by René Privat. He attacked immediately and
left me struggling, as Nencini of Italy joined me. He led me
over the top where we were caught by the main group and
that was the end for me. Privat managed to stay clear and
win, but I had no strength left and got very cross thinking

about my mistake in the distance, for, had I been right, I would have won.

Brian Robinson by now had rented an apartment in Paris, and we left Italy to move in and buy furniture. I spent a pleasant few days there getting a wardrobe and other items and got a great kick out of actually living in the French captial. Our flat was in the Porte de Clichy area and we were very much 'Frenchmen' at that time.

Next came Paris–Roubaix and the dreaded 'Hell of the North' over the rough, uneven cobbles of Belgium. I had read, as a young lad, of the exploits of the famous riders in this gruelling ride and knew that the great Coppi had broken away on this race with another rider. I knew that I, too, would have to do the same but, because I was young and still impulsive, I was determined to ensure that no-one went with me when I made my effort.

At Monsenpevel, which is on a hill, I attacked as the race entered the rough part with 44 kilometres to the finish on the Roubaix track. I went away so fast that I was a minute clear in 10 kilometres, and was told afterwards that I was riding faster than Roger Riviere did when he broke the world hour record.

The surface was terrible. Just imagine a cobbled road built about 150 years ago when Napoleon was on the march, which had never been repaired and had had heavy lorries and tractors over it countless numbers of times. It wound its way through small villages and beet fields and was a succession of ruts and holes over which no self-respecting motorist would ever take his car.

This was a historic event in many ways, for it was being televised live for the first time on the Eurovision link. It was indeed the first cycle race ever to be given this treatment and the TV people used a helicopter and cameramen mounted on motor-cycles to follow the event. I am told that

I occupied the screens in countless homes all over the Continent that day for no less than 56 minutes, in what was termed 'The lone epic'.

But it was not my day. I was caught just three kilometres from the finish by Cerami of Italy and the Frenchman, Sabaddini. They jumped me and went on. As I reached the entrance to the stadium I was caught again by a group of six and passed once more. I had nothing left and so finished in ninth place. People all over France and Belgium wept for me that day, but because of my performance, I was given a bouquet and told to do a lap of honour. I shall always remember the tremendous ovation the packed stadium gave me, for it seems that I had captured the imagination of countless thousands with my impulsiveness and determination. But for me it was a difficult job trying to smile as I rode round, waving to the crowd, for I was so tired and near to tears after being so close to victory. Louviot was almost beside himself and said that he was to blame for my defeat, as he should have come up to tell me of the chasers instead of staying back with Riviere, who was then our best rider.

The publicity was enormous and I felt I had really become famous overnight. The fact that I was living in Paris also made an impact and some of the French magazines tried to turn me into a 'Major Thompson', the mythical Englishman in a famous book written by a Frenchman some years before. They took pictures of me in a bowler hat, and other shots of me reading *The Times*.

I was now on the road to success and was offered more good contracts to ride in events. With my confidence at full strength, plus the thrill of being in the public eye, I developed a sort of 'character', remembering the tips about making people laugh which Hassenforder had given. I enjoyed every minute of it and was glad to have justified the

faith of my friends, although I did not forget that I had not
yet reached the peak.

Not long after the Paris–Roubaix I won the Grand Prix
Mont Faron, a big mountain climb, beating the Luxembourg rider, Charly Gaul, and several other renowned
'grimpeurs'[1]. From there I went into the five-day Tour
of the South East, and it was here that Louviot proved to
me just what a great Directeur Sportif he was. He told me
before the start that I could win, but I did not believe him.

I had kept fairly close to the race leadership for the whole
event, and then on the final day, when my position was
only some two minutes in arrears of the jersey-holder, Louviot gave me my instructions. We were riding into Marseilles
for the finish and already that morning a break had gone
ahead containing Privat and Cazala of the Mercier team,
with Mastrotto of our own squad. At Toulon they had gained
a lead of about six minutes on the field and it was then that
Louviot told me to attack on a climb going out of the
town.

He said that if I waited till then and conserved my
strength he knew I could win. He had more confidence than
I had but I had faith in him and did as I was told. I got
clear with three other team men and two members of the
Mercier team went with us. Louviot went ahead up the
road and told Mastrotto not only to stop working with the
other two, but to wait for us. Poor Mastrotto did not like this
a bit, but Louviot threatened him with not giving him a ride
for the next few months, and the Frenchman literally
stopped at the roadside to wait.

It was not long before we came along and we had, by then,
pulled back two minutes of the deficit. The 'jersey' was back
in the bunch well behind, but it was now Privat that we
had to pull back for his four minutes put him in the overall

[1] Mountain climbers.

lead. We fairly threshed along the road to Marseilles, attempting virtually the impossible, for there were now less than 20 miles to the finish.

We did not catch Privat, who won the stage with his partner, Cazala, taking second place, but I crossed the line third and, with only some two minutes' difference, had won overall! I do not know who was more delighted, Louviot or myself, but he was decidedly happy and told me that this was some recompense for my hard luck in Paris–Roubaix.

This enhanced my position in the racing world, and I earned yet more contracts from this success. About this time I had signed a contract to ride in the Isle of Man international event, just before the Tour de France, and was looking forward to riding once more in England, but I heard a number of rumours that the authorities were after my blood over my call-up, and at the last moment I decided not to go. This was one occasion when my impulse was on my side and it was just as well because I found out later that the Military Police met the 'plane on arrival there, but, for once, the bird had not flown.

Not long afterwards I was fined £25 by the British Federation for failing to appear and breaking my contract, but I considered the sum was well worth it as it saved me from eighteen months National Service. Here again I must point out that I had not wished to dodge anything and it really was force of circumstance which made me act as I did. I know some misguided people in England had been after me and writing to the authorities in order to stir things up. I hope they got some small satisfaction in reading about my defeats in events on the 'other side', after all the hard work they did in trying to get my career ruined.

I only hope that the National Service people look upon this with a kindly eye. Since I have been back in England

on a number of occasions without being arrested or having
had my papers thrust upon me, I presume that everything is
now in order and that I shall not suddenly find myself mar-
ching about some barrack square when I am 40 years old!

# 11

# The Big Tour

MUCH against the advice of M. Louviot I thought I would ride the Tour de France. He was dead against it, making it clear that he thought it was stupid for me to enter as I was much too young. Encouragement from other sources made me finally decide to accept the invitation to join the British team, as the Tour was for national teams that year instead of the normal professional squads. I might add, of course, that Louviot was to prove right as I should not have attempted it so soon, but my impulsiveness or cockiness (take your choice) was at work once more.

This race, which covers around 2,600 miles in 22 days, is not only the supreme test for the bike rider, but is the toughest and most gruelling sporting event in the world. There is nothing to compare with it anywhere and it was to be an ordeal the like of which I have never experienced, before or since.

The first day took us from Lille to Brussels over about 80 miles, and I was soon at the front with a small breakaway group. There were fourteen of us and, unluckily, I finished 13th. As we entered the stadium entrance just short of the line, a rider hit the concrete wall and cannoned off on to me, knocking me over too. I was not hurt much, just a few scratches, and so felt reasonably content with my first showing. But this was only the morning stage, for we had an individual time trial of about 20 miles to ride in the afternoon.

Robinson and I had our meal and then stretched out on the grass outside the track for a nap. It was a warm day and we soon nodded off. We were awakened by the team masseur, and only just in time for the start! There was no chance of a warm-up to get our legs going, for it was a case of grabbing the bike and getting to the line. This was a bad blunder for me as I was the fastest man on the return trip and, had I had a warm-up before the start I could possibly have done a much better ride and might even have taken the lead. As it was I was well placed, lying 6th only a short distance in time away from the leader.

The next day saw us on the road to Dunkirk, where I tried and failed to get away several times early on. The pace was very fast indeed and almost at the Belgian frontier the famous Spaniard, Bahamontes, retired, unable to stand the speed and the rough roads. As we approached the frontier I was being protected by 'Robbo' as I was the best British placed rider and we had just crossed into France when I found that I had a slow puncture.

Very quietly I said to Brian, 'Puncture!' and he replied: 'Take it easy and slip to the back of the bunch.' We manœuvred our way to the rear where I jumped off, pulled out the front wheel and handed it to Robinson. He gave me his rear wheel in return! I had not said which wheel it was and he had assumed it was the back one! Anyway, we quickly rechanged wheels and I was off up the road and soon on again with Robbo coming on shortly afterwards.

At Ostend, I made another attack and this time succeeded, taking with me eight other riders. It was then that a thing happened which I had never imagined. There were three members of the French national team in the break and they would not share the work. Luckily some of the French regional riders were willing to have a go, and we soon held a lead of about $1\frac{1}{2}$ minutes on the bunch. At this point history was made for me as I was the leader of the Tour de France as it stood at that moment on the road.

It was not long before a chase was on behind us with practically the whole Italian team towing the rest of the field. This pulled back our lead to some 50 seconds when there was less than 10 miles to go. The riders from the French national team, who had been having an easy ride, now began to attack off the front. First Grazcyk, then Privat and then Mastrotto would go, each one flying away as we pulled back the other. Obviously it could not go on like this and eventually, with less than two miles to the line, Privat got clear and won by about ten seconds with Jean Grazcyck— blast him!—sitting on my wheel as we came in for the sprint and coming off it to edge me out for second place.

If I had got that second position I would have had the 30 seconds time bonus awarded this placing and thus would have taken over the yellow jersey, for I was only 24 seconds behind the leader. I was not too worried though for second place overall was still pretty marvellous and my spirits were very high.

Apart from Robinson, the other members of the British team, game as they were, were finding it a hard ride and John Kennedy, Harry Reynolds, Vic Sutton, Jock Andrews, Stan Brittain and my old rival and friend Norman Shiel, were lasting out more on sheer guts than anything else. I am not decrying their efforts in any way at all for I think, in the circumstances, they rode magnificently, but it is not an easy thing to come from the more steady riding of Britain into such a hard race as this.

I was still going well and in terrific form all down the west coast of France where, during the following days before the mountains, I conserved myself a bit. I lost a few placings but was quite content, knowing that the climbs were coming,

and that I would again pull up here. I still remember the day
we rode into Bordeaux where the last 56 kilometres were
covered within an hour! Everyone was screaming along with
both the French and Belgian national teams going full blast
at the front.

After just over a week of this type of riding, we arrived in
the Pyrenees, where I was looking forward to moving up in
the general classification. I felt very fit still and rode well on
that first day among the cols and climbed well. I could not
say the same about my descending, however, for I crashed
on the descent of the Aubisque, but only received a few
scratches and bumps. By that night I was feeling very well
and content at the way things had gone for me and was beginning to think that the Tour de France was no different
to any other big stage race.

I had moved up a little in the overall placings as a result
of that mountain stage, and was ready to do battle again as
we set off to climb the mighty Peyresourde. What happened
I shall never know, but I cracked on the ascent and from
that moment it was sheer hell. I had gone into the attack
about halfway up the climb and was holding Nencini's wheel
with Riviere hanging on to mine. Quite suddenly I began
to feel bad. I hung on desperately for as long as I could, my
head started to swim and I felt as though I would burst. My
breathing became laboured and I could not gulp in air
fast enough and I had that almost asphyxiated feeling that
had got me on the Melbourne track in the 1956 Olympics.

There was nothing I could do but slow down. I was only
about a kilometre from the summit but lost three minutes
there as I crawled to the top with the rest of the field going
by me and disappearing over the brow. On the descent I
thought I might feel better, but no! All the energy had been
drained from me and I lost more time on the descent into
Luchon and the finish.

At the hotel I felt terribly ill and utterly exhausted. I did not feel like food and went straight to bed. I slept like a log but felt little better next morning, and was not looking forward to the ride to Toulouse. I just could not understand why I should have suddenly broken down like that and had no idea at all as to what could have made me feel that way. No idea then, but later I began to realise that something quite serious had affected me.

I do not know to this day what it was, but I had my suspicions someone had been meddling with my feeding bottle. No matter how tired I had been in events before I had always recovered well after sleep and certainly had never felt like that.

But that did not help me at all as I struggled painfully along the road to Toulouse. We lost another member of the team here, when Harry Reynolds crashed and broke his collarbone. Great Britain were now down to four men I think, but my recollections, apart from the odd incident, have become very hazy indeed here.

I lost time again on this stage as I was with a small group which had hardly anyone in it who wanted to work. Even at that particular stage there were some who watched me and still counted me as a danger man. I obviously must have looked better than I felt and they little realised that I was to lose some more places before the end.

Those last ten days were agony and ridden almost on willpower alone. Robinson tried to help with words of encouragement, but I was past help and just could not be bothered to listen. He could not give me any assistance during the race now for he was 26th and our best placed rider, and I had to fend for myself.

Three days to go and one of those silly things happened which if things had been all right would not have mattered at all, but because of my condition, seemed so cruel and

senseless. It occurred just before the start of a stage and I
was standing holding my bike and talking to one of the
British journalists, Jock Wadley. Robbo was riding down
the road and, for some unknown reason, something that
cannot be explained, thought that I was riding and crashed
into my stationary machine. The force of it and the fact
that I was not expecting such a thing, sent me to the ground
with a bang. My hands were on the 'bars and so, as I fell
across the bike, I hit my face on the road.

The bike was in quite a mess and we had to do an awful
lot of running about to get it repaired and ready for the
start. Poor Brian was most apologetic and I suppose it was
not really anyone's fault, just one of those stupid accidents,
but it did not help either my condition or my feelings at
the time!

I thought the race would never end and only concentrated
now about Paris and the finish. I had to get there, I must
get there, I kept telling myself, literally forcing myself along
the road. I had lost a lot of weight by now and the scars on
my face from my silly fall had mingled with some sores
which had broke out around my mouth.

I was in a sorry state that final day as I rode into the Parc
des Princ to finish my first Tour. As far as I was concerned
at that moment I had done it. I had lasted this hellish ride
and could say that I had ridden and finished the Tour de
France and I never wanted to ride another one.

The one redeeming feature about the Parc was that
Helen Sherburn was there to meet me and what a shock the
poor girl had when she saw her skinny, scarfaced, sore-
mouthed wreck of a boy-friend! I really did look bad,
though, and had lost nearly two stone in weight over the
three weeks of the race.

It was lovely to see her again but it was to be only for
a very short time, as I had to race once more on the following

night at Evreux in Normandy. I came back from there in time to see her off on the train to Germany and then went to Milan.

I was still very tired, but had recovered my fitness a little. If I could have rested then perhaps I would have felt fine in a few days, but I had to fulfil my contracts to ride in various events.

This is the biggest drawback for a young rider trying to make a name for himself. He rides hard and well to make people notice him and thus gain contracts to ride. Having done this, he then has to work even harder in order to ensure that he stays in the public eye. If you begin to turn down contracts you rarely get a second opportunity to ride that particular event.

Thus, having slogged your guts out to get somewhere, you have to work even more desperately if you want to keep at the top and retain your reputation. So it was with me, and I had to go through with all the contracts, for to break them would not only have meant loss of money but also prestige and I would have been regarded as unreliable.

This vicious circle had me dragging myself round the criterium events at Milan, Turin, Sallanches in the French Alps, and then across to Lyons all within the space of a week after the Tour ended. And that was not all, for I then went to Belgium for a few days of races in different parts of the country, and then made a supreme effort to reach Nice in time for another event.

I had borrowed a car and drove all the way. I finished the race in Belgium late, which gave me only 26 hours to reach Nice—about a thousand miles away. I drove alone and, exhausted, arrived just in time to change and run with my bike to the start line. Three miles was enough for me and I had to retire. I just could not move my legs any more. After a short rest I drove many miles into Central France

for yet another criterium and here, thank goodness, a crash
stopped me.

The circuit was a dangerous one with several pile-ups
and I came down with quite a wallop when my front tyre
blew off. Had I been my usual fit self, I would have just had
a wheel change and ridden on, but this time it was too much
for me to take and I abandoned. I was absolutely dead beat!

# 12

# My Fair Lady

I RETURNED to Paris and the apartment, but on my own, as Robinson was away riding, feeling dispirited and lonely. After only a day there I had an awful feeling of despondency creeping over me and so I decided I was ready for the doctor. I went round to one of the big Parisian hospitals that morning for a check-up and to have my dressings changed by the local Red Cross, who looked after me when I crashed.

As I lay on the couch receiving the once-over, I suddenly thought it would be just the job if I stayed in there for a week. So I took a private ward and had the best service and attention in the hospital! The doctors used to come in for a chat about racing, for I was well-known through the press and I was never lonely and gradually began to feel more like my old self. Helen sent me a home-made fruit cake from Germany and Robbo brought it round from the flat and we had a good chat together. He took over my contracts and so I did not let too many people down. One day while I was lying there, I heard a lot of banging going on in another wing of the hospital. I did not take much notice until I heard the noise of police sirens all over the place, and suddenly there were gendarmes everywhere. The troubles with Algeria were going on then, and I found out that the noise I had heard was machine guns! Two men had rushed into a ward and shot and killed another two men who, poor devils, were lying in bed. Charming! I thought, and was very glad that I had paid for a private ward!

After about a week I felt much better and with my battery recharged to some degree, I went off to the World Championships which that year were round the Saxon Ring in Germany. I did not want to ride in the pursuit, for I was by no means on good form, but was expected to compete in the road race and, who knows? I thought, I might do well. As it turned out I need not have bothered, for another stupid accident put me out.

I had covered about four laps of the circuit when a shoe lace broke and my foot came straight out of the shoe. I slowed down and eased off the back of the field and stopped to put matters right. I heard a car behind me somewhere, but did not take very much notice of it until I heard the brakes being applied, when I tried to move out of the way. I was too late and I was given a sharp bump which sent me over the bike and down on to the road—with my head making contact first!

Five stitches were inserted in the injury and then I received quite a telling off from M. Louviot, who told me it was all my fault and I should look where I am and at what is happening. I think he was right too, he usually was, for I was not really paying attention to detail.

So, back to France I went to fulfil a few more contracts. I did not do anything much as I was still tired and rather fed up. For the first time in my life I had had enough cycling and was no longer interested in it.

Earlier I had bought a second-hand Aston Martin D.B.2 —a 1953 model—which had needed some repairs to it. It was ready now and I could think of no better thing to do than to drive to Stuttgart and see Helen. As cycling had gradually gone out of my head, Helen had filled it, and she was very much in my thoughts over those last couple of

months. By now the year was nearly over and it was late
November when I spent a very pleasant time with her,
thanks to the kindness of the family she stayed with, for they
gave her a lot of time off. I had not been able to go to her
21st birthday as I was racing, but we both enjoyed my own
23rd at the end of the month.

I left for England and home on the following day and
felt as happy as a man could. I was able now to take things
easy for a while. I had a car, I was going home for Christmas and Helen would be there too for she was leaving Germany on the 22nd December. Also I was returning to see
my parents, and a special occasion as well, for I was to be
'best man' at the wedding of one of my old friends, Bill
Womack.

I drove back, enjoying my car, and took the road from
Dover without a care in the world. As I was approaching
Newark I noticed there was a big traffic hold-up going into
the town. I knew Newark from my early cycling days and
realised that the level-crossing gates were closed. This was
before the by-pass had been built, and, impatient to get
home, I swung the wheel over and drove along the right
hand side of the road, past the big queue of traffic.

I reasoned that by the time I reached the gates they would
be opening and I would be able to slip in somewhere and
knew that no traffic would be coming the other way. I should
have known that my luck was not that good, and as I approached the gates they were still firmly shut. I slowed down,
and as I got near to the front of the line I saw, to my horror,
a police car was second in the line. I pulled the left-hand
drive Aston Martin to a stop alongside the black Wolseley,
and pretending not to notice, stared straight ahead, feeling
my face going slightly red at the same time!

The driver wound down his window and pushed his head
out towards me. 'What do you think you're doing?' he asked,

crossly. 'Don't you realise you are on the wrong side of the
road?' Using my hands expressively, I turned to him and
replied 'Non!' He took a quick look at my left-hand drive
and said, 'Another bloody froggie!' and waved me on as the
gates opened. Phew! I was glad he had not asked for my
passport!

I had a very nice time at home going round and visiting
all my friends and showing off the car. I was relaxed and
feeling really well again, and looking forward to Helen
coming home, for it would be the first time we had been together in England, although we had known each other for
nearly two years.

We became engaged on Christmas Eve, and on the day
after Boxing Day, my impulsiveness taking over, I took her
off to the church and asked the Vicar how soon he could
marry us! I knew that Helen had to go back to Germany
early in the New Year and that I would be racing again, and
felt that we should not wait until the next autumn which
would have been the first opportunity we would have had.
The Vicar was very good and said we could get married on
the following Thursday, the 3rd January.

Thereupon everybody began rushing around trying to get
things done in time. It was not exactly a 'secret' wedding,
but there were only about nine close friends and our families
in the know because there was not very much time to do
anything in the way of laying on a reception and all that
palaver.

We bought the ring in Sheffield on the Saturday, and
Helen got herself a suit. We drove then to Helen's Uncle
Frank and Aunt Cora, who lived, at that time, in Chester-
field. We could not tell them, of course, which was pretty
awful really and I was trying to pull Aunt Cora's leg about
it, saying that I had a secret and she was going on about
what she would wear at the wedding and when were we

going to name the day! She wanted to see the suit Helen
had bought and I was whistling away 'I'm getting married
in the morning' from *My Fair Lady,* but the penny never
dropped. They were both very disappointed when we told
them afterwards, but understood and were so nice about it
all. I always refer to them as my favourite Aunt and Uncle
now!

The great day came and went without a hitch. One of
the main reasons for our silence about the wedding was the
Press, as I had received quite a bit of publicity in the English
newspapers that year, one way or another, which, incidentally, was a refreshing change. Thus we had not wanted to
engage a photographer in case he had let on and my father-
in-law took the wedding pictures with an old box camera!

Gerald O'Donovan, a Director of Carlton Cycles, was
my best man, and after the ceremony we all went back to
my in-laws' home for a few drinks and a slice of wedding
cake. This, by the way, had been a Christmas cake only a
short while before and the greetings had been hurriedly
scraped off the top and replaced by a model bride and
groom!

We left almost immediately for London, as I had been invited to the *Daily Mirror* Sportsmans' Dinner. This was
amusing for they had asked me if I was going to bring a
friend so that rooms could be booked etc., and I had to reply
on a special form. Well, I could not put down my wife because this would have let the cat out of the bag, so I just
put down for a double room with my name and that of Miss
Helen Sherburn! We had quite a laugh at the hotel, which
we found by asking a taxi driver to lead us there. We were
shown up to the room where there were two single beds
just about as far away from each other as they could possibly
be!

Going into London I thought it would be nice to call in

and see my sister Alice and tell her the news. She had heard about Helen, of course, but had never seen her. After the usual introductions I said to her, 'We're married, you know, Alice.' There was a short silence and then my sister replied, 'Now look here, Tom, are you pulling my leg?'

Naturally she believed us in the end, but I had quite a laugh about it for I am sure she thought I was just saying it so that I might get a chance to sleep with Helen, Alice having assumed we wanted to stay the night!

There were more surprises in store for people at the Dinner and the first one I told was Brian Robinson. He did not believe me either and it finally took Helen to convince him by showing her wedding ring to him. He was very kind and talked away to me like a father. He went on, 'Now then, Tom lad, be careful. You've a career to think of and you mustn't go having children straightaway.' And so on. I felt I knew best about what I wanted to do, but thanked him anyway, for it was very genuine and I really did appreciate his concern.

The secret was out now, of course, but it did not matter any more and we had a very pleasant evening at the Dinner. The next day we were off to Paris, where we stayed at the apartment. There was not very much time for us to get to know married life, however, since we had only four days together. On the 8th January I put Helen on the train for Germany and then went down to the training camp at Narbonne.

Here I worked hard and was, of course, an entirely different man. Relaxed, content, happily married, what more could I need with a bright future ahead of me as a professional bike rider? I enjoyed being back on the bike again and the time passed quickly enough.

I was soon back in Paris again in readiness to start the Paris–Nice event, and Helen had now finished her spell

in Stuttgart, returning 'home' at about the same time as my
arrival. We spent a short time there before the start of the
race and then, as on so many occasions in later years, we were
to be separated again for a time.

Paris–Nice proved to be a good race for me as I finished
fifth overall, having taken things quite steadily right through
the event. I could feel all my old form surging back and within a few days had done another good ride in Milan–San
Remo. Still not exerting myself too much, I found that I
was probably going better than I had ever done before and
I felt fitter, happier and more confident than I had done
for a long time. Still in Italy I rode the Genoa–Rome stage
race and ended second overall. I could have won, but Geldermans, of our own team, had had the lead and so, as a
good professional should, I rode for him throughout the
race. What had been a highlight for me was my win in the
time trial stage when I beat Anquetil. This was a great moment, as the Frenchman is reckoned to be the best at this
type of racing and I had a lot of satisfaction from the victory.
I then flew from Rome to Brussels and on to Ghent for the
start of the single-day classic, the Tour of Flanders. I was
determined that I would win it for, over the previous few
weeks, I had never really extended myself and was certain
that I could beat anybody. Of course I had had that sort
of feeling many times before in my life, and quite often
things did not turn out the way I expected. But the Tour of
Flanders was different.

# 13

# Hard Going

THE Tour of Flanders starts and finishes in the Ghent area, and in fact the finish that year, 1961, was at Wetteren. The usual class field had entered and, completely in top form, I was ready for anything. I attacked only twice in the race and each time they were winning moves. I felt so good during and after the event that I class this victory as probably one of the finest rides I have ever done.

I had sat in for a while, biding my time and observing what was happening, and with 60 miles to the finish, I attacked. A small group of riders were already away at the front and it was not long before I joined them. Only the Italian road champion, Defilippes, got my wheel as I left the bunch and it was that same rider who went with me later again.

We had all worked hard in the breakaway group, and with the finish getting nearer, I decided that with five miles to go, I must attack again. We were now on the finishing loop section which goes over the finishing line three times. In other words, you do three laps before sprinting for the line.

I got clear, dragging Defilippes with me, and we were soon up the road leaving the others to sort out their own fate. As we rode on round this finishing section, I had no qualms at all about the Italian. He was probably one of the best roadman sprinters in the world at that time, and yet, somehow or other, I knew I could beat him. I knew also that it would be a sprint between us for I realised he was too strong for me to drop him over the short distance that remained.

I started my sprint about a kilometre from the line, and as I anticipated, Defilippes took my wheel. I had worked out just what I was going to do and it went like a charm! With some 300 metres to go I feigned that I had 'blown up' and slowed slightly. Immediately the Italian took a flyer off my wheel and passed me on my right, going like a train for the line. As he went I restarted sprinting, really going flat out, and drew almost alongside him on his right. I reasoned that he would look back to see where I was, and since he had gone by me on the right, would look to his left for me. He did just that, and got the shock of his life for I was nowhere in sight! In the split second it took him to turn his head to the opposite side, I went past him. He had slowed momentarily through being taken by surprise like that, and I was over the line just a wheel in front of him!

There was pandemonium! He just could not believe he had been beaten, especially by me, since I had not, at that time, been regarded as a great sprinter. Immediately he lodged a protest that he did not see the line properly—that there was no finish banner marking it out. This was true, for a very high wind that day had blown the banner down, but we had crossed that line three times previously and there was no doubt that he knew where it was!

The attention then turned to the line itself—it was not clearly marked out and difficult to see, and so it went on. The officials remained firm, and the result upheld. But even that was not the end of it for some of the journalists started to stir things up, particularly those from the Italian papers. The next thing I knew was that the Italians came to see me and asked me if I would agree to an 'equal first' decision. Not on your life! They told me that an Italian had not won a classic since 1953, but I replied that an Englishman had not won one since 1896! I was not to be talked into or out of anything. It was my victory and I had won it and no one was going to share the honour. By Gum! I was not going to let anyone take away my first classic win!

So the result remained and into the record books went my name, the first Britisher to win the Tour of Flanders. Gradually the hue and cry subsided, but it was weeks before the papers and the people stopped writing and talking about it. It was then and only then that I realised just how important a classic victory really was. This is difficult to explain in a way, but nothing I had ever done before, in all my good rides, counted like this. Everybody wanted me for interviews on the radio and television and I felt I was a star.

Helen did not know that I had won and was back in the apartment in Paris when a woman from another flat ran to tell her the news. Helen was not able to appreciate the importance of my success, but began to understand when the neighbour was so excited about it.

She realised it even more when I rushed into the flat and told her to get her coat on quickly as we were both going to be interviewed on the television! She wanted to know why she too was on the interview and that was answered quite simply. They wanted to know how she had made me a champion. She had, of course, to some degree, done just this and I was no longer Tom Simpson, the English cyclist, I was Tom Simpson of Great Britain, the classic winner.

Still feeling good and with my success giving me more confidence and speed, I rode the Paris–Roubaix, the scene of the do-or-die lone break that brought me so much attention in the previous year. In the 'hell of the north' I broke away again with the Frenchman, Poulidor, after me.

I was determined that he should not reach me for I wanted to ride alone, as I had done before, and I knew, anyway, that I could ride the faster. We had ridden at a very fast pace, and because of this had caught up with some of the race cars in front. The police were trying like the devil to get them out of the way, but on the rough, narrow, twisting road it was impossible.

The cars now began to impede my progress and, as I tried to get by on one section of road, a Press car pulled over and forced me into a ditch. My front wheel was smashed and I received a number of bumps, including one on my knee which, although not worrying me much at the time, was to give me a lot of trouble later on.

The wheel changed, I went on but the Paris–Roubaix is perhaps the hardest race to win when you are at the rear. After a few more miles I punctured. Another hold-up resulted and eventually I came into the stadium nearly half an hour down.

This was not as bad as in Italy once. I arrived at the track so far behind that everyone had gone! The doors were all locked and there I was, like a lost sheep. I had to get a taxi-driver to take me and my bike to the hotel. I felt a proper nit, I can tell you!

I went to Spain for the first time and rode in the Grand Prix Eibar, a four-day event run in the Basque region. I had never been in the country before and was not at all impressed, as it poured with rain for the whole four days. Talk about the 'rain in Spain'—it was frightful and the wet and cold started my knee aching.

I was staggered by the way the Spaniards climbed. They were terrific, which was more than could be said of my own performance. My knee did not help and by the time we were into the second day I began to feel ill. All the energy had drained out of me by the next day and I felt stiff and tired and sick. I did not know what was wrong with me but certainly I was most unwell and abandoned the race on the final day.

I broke out in a rash all over my body and by the time I reached home was in quite a state. It was found that I had had food poisoning and the doctors just could not clear up the rash. It persisted for a long time and I saw quite a number of specialists. I recovered slowly and, like an idiot, rode the Tour de France.

It was an absolute disaster for I only lasted three stages and the less said about them the better! Why I rode I do not know, for I was far from fit and my knee was now really hurting and affected my riding. The whole episode from the time I won the Tour of Flanders had changed me completely and I had gone down the hill in a matter of three months. My usually high standard was gone and this was reflected in the fact that I only received seven contracts to ride in criteriums that year.

Of course it did do some good, I suppose, for it gave me time to think why it was I had begun so well and then gone to pieces. I knew that the crash and the injury to my knee had been partly the cause, and the food poisoning had done me no good, but even so, I could, no, I *should* have been better.

I decided that I was looking at things from the wrong angle. I knew that it was not difficult to get to the top, it was staying there once the summit had been reached. Thus I realised that I would have to set my stall out differently in the future and straightaway set about having my knee put to rights.

It was still very bad and I saw a number of specialists without very much success. Heat treatment, ointments and all sorts of poultices were tried but to no avail. Eventually I went to see Dr. Creff at St. Michael's Hospital in Paris. He was an athletic consultant and also interested himself in cyclists and was a very well-known figure.

He had written a number of books about various injuries to athletes and their treatments and soon had me to rights. He started by giving me injections in the knee, and within a month I was feeling much more like my old self.

I went into strict training and worked hard, intending to have another try at the World Championships. They were held in Switzerland that year and so Helen and I went there just before the 'worlds' and spent a fortnight's camping holiday which we both enjoyed tremendously.

Once more I tried my hand at the pursuit and qualified with the fourth fastest time. In the quarter finals I came up against Peter Post of Holland and out I went. This time, though, the beating did not worry me as much as some of my defeats in earlier days, and I was reasonably content with things, for I knew that I was not in top condition.

I did a bit more thinking to myself here for I saw that pursuiting had changed from when I was really going great guns at it as an amateur. The general rule was to get in a fast lap or two and then ease slightly and get one's second wind, as it were, before starting the final few laps again very fast. Now it was 'go, go, go' all the time, and like athletics, the men were pushing themselves further all the time. I knew that if the style had altered then so must I and, therefore, had to develop more speed and skill if I was to beat the rest.

The following week I rode in the World Championship road race. I had not trained properly for this but decided that the distance might do me some good. The holiday had made me feel much better and I was physically fit, if not cycling fit.

It was not a very exciting event. I found it rather boring, in fact, but managed to get with the important break when

it went and, considering my lack of miles, rode quite well
and certainly better than I had anticipated.

There were about 17 of us in this group and I was placed
ninth in the final sprint, which was won by Van Looy who
had also won the title the year before. The most eventful
happening in the whole race took place right there at the
finish, for, only a few metres from the line, Van Looy's rear
wheel began to collapse. As he crossed the line his gears
were scraping along the road and he must have thanked his
lucky stars it had not happened earlier.

Soon afterwards I learned that Helen was going to have
a baby. We were both absolutely delighted, and, as I said
then, 'At least if I cannot ride a bike it shows that I can do
something properly!' Naturally there were immediate problems for we needed somewhere to live. Our apartment was
too small and anyway there were 110 steps to climb to it.

We were not in a very good financial state either, as I
had not won very much and had not been getting the contracts owing to my early season illnesses. It was difficult too,
trying to borrow money or get a loan in France as I was a
foreigner and, in any case, had no security to offer.

I thought about moving elsewhere and asked a friend of
ours, Ken Dockray, who owned a garage in Ghent, if he
would look out for any property that might be going in
that area. We then had a magnificent stroke of luck. Ken
found out that one of his customers, M. René Hailliez, who
owned some properties in the town, had a small house available and would be most pleased if we would take it.

M. Hailliez was most kind and generous to us for he
hardly charged us any rent at all, which was an absolute
godsend, especially as things turned out. Naturally we jumped at the chance and moved into Belgium and Ghent at the
beginning of October.

Albert Beurick, ever helpful, brought his van down to

Paris and so we moved our various bits and pieces in that and the car. We had quite a time at the frontier, however, because I made a stupid mistake and forgot to declare a radio. The Customs men turned everything out of the car and the van and so we had a long and boring wait while they went over all our worldly goods!

We stayed at Albert's place, the Café den Engel, for about a week, while the cottage was put into order, and then we were in our new home. Money was a big problem still for I had spent just about all I had in getting things for the home and my savings from racing over the more successful periods had virtually gone. Thus it was only the generosity of M. Hailliez that saved us from serious financial trouble. I had tried, unsuccessfully, to get a few contracts, but managed to gain some interest from the indoor track promoters for I landed a few engagements to ride in Ghent, Brussels and Antwerp. My luck then, I thought, may be turning at last and looked forward to 1962 with a lighter heart.

# 14

# Getting Around Europe (the Hard Way)

AT THE end of the 1961 season Jacques Anquetil joined the St. Raphael team. This was not to my liking at all for, while I had nothing personal against him, he was a great rider and, as such, would receive all the attention. I knew that some day, despite my present difficulties, I too would be at the top, and therefore did not wish to ride for Anquetil for the rest of my days.

I felt that I stood a better chance elsewhere and let it be known that I was on the market, as it were. In any case my contract with St. Raphael had not been renewed for the 1962 season and, due to my poor showing that year, I rather doubted their wanting me! As things turned out it did not matter too much, for I received an offer to join the Gitane–Leroux team which I naturally accepted.

I started training with my new team mates in early February at Lodève in the South of France, and soon began to feel on good form again. My first race was to be Paris–Nice, where I really turned things on and finished second, behind the Belgian, Joseph Planckaert.

I was flying again now and my spirits soared but I became terribly disappointed when I could not ride Milan–San Remo. The organisers had decided that only Italian professional teams could ride the race and so I could not enter. I had really looked forward to this and honestly believed that I could have won.

Denied the opportunity of winning that particular classic I turned my attention to the Tour of Flanders. I rode very well, finishing fifth in a small breakaway and taking the 'King of the Mountains' title. It was this race which made people begin to realise that I was a good rider and my win the previous year had not been a fluke. They knew in that race that it was only the team tactics employed by the winner, Van Looy, who had three members of his team in that break, which prevented me from gaining another victory. Then I was off again in the Paris–Roubaix and still on very good form. I got with the 'paying' break of the day and finished well up behind the winner, again the irrepressible Van Looy. By now it was April and our baby was due soon so I arranged for Helen to go to England to stay with her parents for the event. I moved down to the Toulon area to race and spent a lot of money and time telephoning to England every other day.

No news and No news was beginning to make me even more tense and excited and when I telephoned them on a Friday three times and got no reply, I assumed that they had all gone out for the day. The following day I was having lunch before going out to take a look at the course for a mountain race I was in on the Sunday, and suddenly saw in the French papers that I was the father of a girl, Jane!

Well, that put me on top of the world and I rushed off to book myself a flight from Paris. I had to ride the race, but my excitement offered no additional aid and I punctured anyway and finished with the big bunch. I caught the night train to the French capital and was soon home.

With the greatest possible pleasure and delight I saw my

lovely little girl—and my lovely big girl too! Helen was fine and Janie, while being absolutely terrific, was rather small. I remember saying to Helen, 'Is that all there is?' But she was smashing! I had only time for three days in England and so was soon off again, taking Helen and Janie, with my mother coming over to Ghent as well to help out for a time.

I was still riding well and was placed in various events but still could not win. Then came the Tour of Luxembourg, a four-day event, and I was flying again. I got the 'jersey' and, like an idiot, attacked and broke away on the third day instead of sitting in and taking things easy. Planckaert and Armand Desmet of the Solo/Superia team went with me and, impulsive as ever, I fought them all the way.

It really was a stupid thing to do for it is not easy to ride against two men. By Gum! They bloody well hammered me that day for I rode myself into the ground in trying to match their constant attacks. I was so shattered that I abandoned before the end of the stage, but I think I did the right thing. I had taken a thrashing so many times in the past and, instead of giving in and resting for a while, had carried on.

I knew that I could get over to England in time to ride in the Isle of Man International and, a rest on the flight, plus an overnight stay, would see me fully recovered, and that is what I did. I lost money on it though for as I had retired in the Luxembourg event, I received no prize money.

Never mind! I became quite excited going over on the 'plane from Paris for it was to be the first time that I had ridden in England as a professional on the road and really looked forward to seeing a few old friends. More than that I wanted to win and reckoned I stood a good chance.

Before the British crowds I went very well and, with only four laps of the circuit to go, I broke away alone. It was not my day though, for the strong wind troubled me and

I was caught on the last lap. The German, Rudi Altig, won the sprint although I was fairly well placed in the leading group. Once more I had come unstuck and was still chasing my first win of the season.

I was very cross about losing, especially as it was my first pro race in England and I felt as though I had let everybody down. Back in France it was time again for 'Le Tour' and I was, this time, looking forward to it for several reasons.

Firstly I was older, a little sadder but a lot wiser. Secondly, I was definitely fitter than I had been for a long time and, lastly, and perhaps most important, the race was back again into trade teams so that I would have some good riders around me. The latter was certainly true for our team captain was André Darrigade who, you will recall, said some nice things about me after the 1959 World Championship. There were several other good, experienced Tour riders with me and our Directeur Sportif was none other than M. Louviot, who had joined Citane–Leroux at about the same time as myself.

The race started from Nancy and I managed to keep with the leading groups for the first week. Just before we reached the mountains we were a very happy team indeed for Darrigade, better known to all his fans as 'Dede', was the holder of the yellow jersey with yours truly right behind him in second place!

Then into the mountains and history. There was a big battle on the cols where many great names came to grief. Darrigade was dropped and I joined up with a group of about 25 riders after we had climbed the Tourmalet, Aspin and Peyresourde with the rest of the field strung out behind.

We finished together and I had the yellow jersey! What a fabulous moment it was and I know people in Britain were pleased for the papers did me proud, but it was nothing to

what happened over in France. They had my pictures
everywhere including one of me in my newly won jersey
complete with bowler hat and umbrella! Shades of Major
Thompson!

That day I received more than the jersey for I got a
monumental telling off from Louviot for not contesting the
sprint at the finish. He said that Geldermans, then only
about half a minute behind me, might have taken the 30-
second time bonus and had the jersey himself. I replied that
I did not want to risk a crash in the bunch sprint and that I
had been watching Geldermans anyway in case he made a
move, but Louviot was annoyed.

Whether this made him do something which he would not
have attempted normally I do not know but I am certain his
decision the following day was wrong. It was perhaps
the only bad piece of judgment he ever made in dealing
with me for he made me ride higher gears for the mountain
time trial the next day.

This was one of the toughest days of the Tour and consisted of the climb at Superbagneres—about 15 miles and
almost straight up! I shall always blame Louviot for my
terrible day there as I just could not get used to the higher
gears he made me ride. My climbing ability has a lot of
rhythm with it and having to change gears frequently
throws me off-balance. This happened that day and I had
not only the distinction of being the first Biritsh rider to
wear the jersey but also was probably the first rider to hold
it for such a short time!

I lost a number of places that day but recovered again
slightly to move into third place overall when we reached
the highest town in Europe, Besançon, on the last Alpine
stage but one. The next day we were on the move to Aix-les-
Bains and here I made a bad mistake which cost me quite
a lot. Descending the Col de Porte at speed I was following

behind a motor-cyclist which I should not have done. My speed was about 50–60 m.p.h. and suddenly, as I rounded a bend where there was a lot of gravel on the road, the machine just skidded away over the edge and I was launched into space!

Fortunately it was not a terribly bad drop but I hit a tree about fifteen feet up its length and then slithered to the ground. My bike was stuck in the branches and one of the French cameramen, who had seen me fly off the road, climbed up and helped me get it down. Miracles will never cease I thought as I climbed up on to the road for it seemed perfectly all right. The wheels were quite in order and I could not find anything wrong at all as I gave it a quick examination.

I jumped on and tore off down the mountain as quickly as I could and found that the machine was too small! What had happened was that it must have hit the tree right on the front which had telescoped it slightly and it was awful to ride as my knees were coming up round my ears! I changed bikes from the team car at the bottom and rode on to the finish with a lot of aches and pains now, including the middle finger of my left hand which was cut and swollen and I could not bend it round the bars.

I was patched up after the stage where they found out I had broken the finger and it was put in plaster. That and my other cuts and bruises, though, did not hurt me so much as having gone down to sixth place! Again the next day was all wrong for me as it was the longest time trial stage of the Tour. This meant that I could get no rest at all in the bunch and so get over the effects of my crash, which had left me very stiff.

So I had to ride alone into Lyons without being able to obtain any benefit from my team mates. I ached all over and it was very difficult to hold the bars properly with the plaster keeping my finger stuck out. I struggled into the finish and retained my sixth position. Anquetil won the stage and there took over the leadership which he held until the end.

I kept my place until the finish although having a rather worrying and, in a way, amusing experience on the last stage into Paris. Some miles from the finish there was a pile-up involving about forty riders and, down I went, landing almost on top of Anquetil. Everybody was all mixed up with each other as is usual in these crashes and I found I had got my plastered up finger stuck in the spokes of the race leader's back wheel! It took me a few moments lying there to extract it and I was pretty glad that someone gave Anquetil another machine and he had not tried to ride away immediately!

I arrived in the Parc des Princ to the tremendous cheers of a small British contingent that had been flown over by *Cycling* magazine. They went wild over me and I felt overjoyed to receive such a reception. My surprises were not over for the day by a long chalk though, for while Helen was there to greet me, so was my mother! She had been flown out specially by the *Daily Express* to see me finish the Tour and was delighted with everything. So was I, of course, and it was a very kind thing to do for us.

Although I had not seen Helen for some time, I did not have long with her, for I was away almost immediately on the contracts 'circus' around the Continent. This is all hard racing with about 500 miles travelling nearly every other day to get to all the places.

Strangely enough I did not feel so tired as I had on the other Tours, big or small, and I began to think that it was because I was getting older and had more stamina. I thought about the race and where I had made my mistakes and resolved to remember these things in the future. All in all, I suppose, it was a good ride, but with more luck and fewer mistakes, I could have had a better position, although I do not think I could have won.

With the contracts ended, I moved off once more to try my luck at the World Championships, held that year in Salo, in northern Italy. I was tired now and not really fit for such a trial of strength and I had certainly not prepared myself properly for such an occasion.

The vital break went away quite early in the race as had happened many times before in world championships. With about 40 miles to go I attacked and got clear. I went too hard early on, again my impulsiveness driving the pedals round too quickly for my physical condition to take. I pulled back a minute in ten miles and soon had them in sight. Could I close that gap? Not on your life! It was one of the most agonising moments of my racing career to sit there and see them only about 50 yards up the road and I just could not get on. I saw no reason to flog myself any further. I had taken so much out of myself already that even if I did get to them I would be too shattered to contest the sprint and I abandoned, feeling very miserable with the realisation that I still had not won a race for a very long time.

I cheered up pretty quickly when Helen told me she was going to have another baby and so, at the end of September, with a few more criterium events under my pedals I turned once more to the indoor tracks.

# 15

# Slipping Down the Ladder

IN EARLY October I was off to Spain to ride the Madrid
Six-day with John Tressider, the Australian. This was to be
my first taste of the 'Sixes' for, although I had ridden the indoor tracks before, I had never gone through the ordeal of
a full six days of hammering round the boards.

In the early days 'Sixes' were terribly hard because the
competitors were expected to ride the whole duration of the
race. This has changed a lot in recent years as the riders
were too tired to show their real paces in front of the crowds.
Since the audience paid the cash, efforts were made to alter
rules in order to keep everyone happy.

While a large number of these events are fairly easy com-
pared with those bygone days, the Madrid 'Six' is still a very
tough one. Trust me to ride the hardest! This race is probably the only one in Europe which requires one rider from
each team (all teams are of two riders) on the track 24
hours a day for the six days. Even during the period from
4 a.m. to 10 a.m., when the race is 'neutralised', which
means that no one can 'steal a lap', a man from each team
must still be there riding round the track.

This particular period is the only one when you can get
any sleep and that is for about three hours while your partner is out pedalling slowly round. Then it is 'all change' and
he gets his rest, such as it is, before everything gets going

again. Six days of this is no joke but believe me, there is an awful lot of fun to be had by both riders and spectators alike, and when I found out that Johnnie Tressider was quite a lad to ride with, I had no shortage of amusing moments.

He was a great partner and, like most Aussies, was a good, tough 'bikie'. The main occupation of all the teams during that race seemed to be to try to find some way to get some extra sleep, which meant dodging the Track Manager, who was a wily character. Our mechanic and general 'runner' was David Nice, an Englishman from Colchester, who had spent the season racing in Belgium and had come down with us to get the atmosphere of a 'six' and to earn himself some money.

Facially he was not unlike me in a way, for his nose appeared to be, profile view anyway, very similar to mine (poor lad!) and I hit on the splendid idea of putting him out on the track in my place during the neutralised period. Tracksuited, a scarf over the lower part of his face and a Russian hat that I had bought, completed the disguise. He was me to anyone giving a cursory glance at the figures plodding round the track.

The get-up was quite in order for it became very cold there at night as they used to turn off all the heating. Everything went well for the first night of the wheeze and I congratulated myself on the plan. It could not go on for ever though, worse luck, for on the very next night the game was up. Dave was trundling round wrapped up to the eyebrows as before when, horrors upon horrors, the Track Manager, who often rode a bike round himself during the quiet time, started to talk to him!

He thought it was me at first and chattered away quite happily to Dave, whose French was near enough non-existent. Well, it was not long before he sensed something was wrong and whipped the scarf off the poor lad's face. He stormed over to my cabin and dragged me out, half asleep, on to the track. That was that! He and the other officials kept their eyes on us after this and we had little chance of getting away with any more larks like that.

Tired, but very happy, we finished the race in third place, both of us feeling in good form despite lack of sleep. We had to get back to Belgium almost immediately for we were due to race in Ghent quite soon and, as soon as our prize money had been given to us we were off on the road. Dave Nice, who had remained awake for practically the whole six days through looking after us, was absolutely dead beat and we put him in the back of the car. It took us about 27 hours to drive back, taking turns at the wheel, and Dave slept all the way. He never saw Spain at all for we had arrived there at night, too, but he did a grand job for us.

In the early part of November we rode together in Brussels and Ghent, mainly in the Madison events. We did quite well in Ghent, and when we went round to collect our money from the organiser he wanted us to sign up for the Six-day there at the end of the month. I was delighted at the chance of earning some more money and did not take long to sign the contract.

In readiness for the event I moved all my quipment, including track bike, into the stadium—the Sportpaleis—before making a quick trip back to England for the Cycle Show at Earls Court. I left early the next morning and got to the Show about lunchtime. I was hardly through the door before I met René de Latour, who sent me cold with shock when he asked me what I knew about the Ghent track being burned down in the night! I just could not believe it at first, but it was true enough. I had a telegram which Helen had sent to one of the stands waiting for me, saying just that. The Sportpaleis had been completely gutted and all my precious stuff, bike and all, had gone with it!

So that was how the 1962 season ended for me—on a hotter note than when it started and I had lost money through the accident, both in terms of my contract and personal belongings. That was not the end of the sad tale either for 1963 had hardly got under way before I found that my contract with Leroux was not going to be renewed. I could hardly blame anyone for not wanting me, after all, I had not won a race since the 1961 Tour of Flanders which was then almost two years ago.

Peugeot were trying to build a stronger team under their Directeur Sportif, Gaston Pläud, and, together with several other riders, I was transferred to their team. I did not get a contract though, I suppose because of my bad record, but I decided to ride for them, mainly because I did not think anyone else would want me! They did pay me some money, although I did not actually sign a contract until the November of that year.

I had managed to save a little money as a result of my good ride in the Tour de France and the ensuing contract rides and, with another baby on the way, Helen and I thought it best if we found a larger home. In any case I felt that I could no longer accept M. Hailliez' generosity and, anyway, someone else was in need of the cottage.

This was Vin Denson who, like myself, had come over to seek his fortune as a professional and was finding things hard. 'Big Vin' was more than large in stature for he has a heart as big as himself and is just about the friendliest man I know on a bike. He and his wife needed somewhere and, once more, M. Hailliez turned up trumps. So we moved to a slightly larger house at Mariakerke on the outskirts of Ghent and made ready for our next arrival.

At this time I had to do a lot of heart-searching for I knew that it was now or never. It was no longer just me, for I had a wife and a family to look after. I was, despite my own thoughts on the matter, nothing more than a second grade professional and had slipped down the ladder badly over a period of just 18 months or so. I knew in myself that if the breaks had come right and luck had been a bit more on my side I would have still been in the big-time but there was little consolation in thinking that way.

I had had a number of good placings, even seconds in big races, but if you want to be a star, and shine at the top, only first place really counts. So I pulled all my resources together and concentrated mentally, first of all, on the advice I had been given in my early years and gradually I talked myself into the right frame of mind.

I was not going to be beaten this time. That was my uppermost thought as I left home for the south and the Peugeot training camp. It was now or never all right and I set about training with a determination that even surprised me! It was not long before I felt my old self and in a matter of weeks I was riding Paris–Nice once more. I did not try to go mad but rode myself in steadily and did a reasonable ride.

Improving all the time I went into the Milan–San Remo where I made one of my silly mistakes. Why I did it I shall never know but I am quite sure that I sacrificed my chance of winning purely because of unselfishness. I really felt good and was away in a break with another Peugeot rider, the West German, Rolf Wolfshohl. I told him I would work for him and gave him the benefit of my knowledge of the course as we went along.

I advised him to attack as we climbed the Poggio hill, only a few miles from the finish, but the clot went away before we reached it and took the little Frenchman, Groussard, with him. Wolfshohl killed everyone off in that attack, including me, and at the finish let Groussard beat him in the sprint! That taught me a lesson though and, while I am always ready to help a team mate, I try to win myself if it is at all possible.

It was March now and from Italy I returned to Belgium for the Ghent–Wevelgem absolutely bang on form. It was a hard, fast race and I attacked a number of times and got clear with a few others, only to be pulled back again. There were quite a few good Belgian sprinters in the field and, at the line, I was beaten by the hair on a gnat's back by Benoni Beheyt, the Belgian, who was, later that year, to become World Champion and raise quite a storm in his own country, but that is another story.

I was furious at losing for I was quite sure that I was the best man that day and the loss only made me more determined to try harder next time. I did try hard but I still could not win. I got third in the Tour of Flanders, did another good ride in the Paris–Roubaix and then went like a bomb in Paris–Brussels.

This, like all the classic events, is a hard, killing ride. It had been said that anyone who broke away before the frontier never won the race. I was out to prove this saying wrong and attacked right at the start. Impulsive? Yes, I suppose I was but it seemed like good tactics and away I went with about 160 miles ahead of me, taking several riders along as well.

As we rode on the lead mounted and, at one time, our group had a 13-minute lead on the bunch! Soon I was left with only Jean Stablinski for company and I could have done without him! The lead dwindled as the main group forced the pace and our own legs began to tire. With two miles to go we were just under a minute clear and I began to smell victory at last.

No such thing! As we climbed the last short ascent on the rough cobbled road I missed a gear change and Stablinski shot away. By the time I had the gear in he was about 20

metres up the road and try as I did I could not pull him
back. So it was another placing but I had really tried and
my name was coming back into the headlines again. The
French were calling me the 'eternal second' and I think, at
that time, nearly everyone wanted to see me win a race.

I knew my win must come soon for I was showing tremendous form and started the Liége–Bastogne–Liége full of confidence. It was not long before I featured in another long
breakaway, this time of about 90 miles and mostly alone.
Two things were wrong about that race and the combination of both of them tended to give me quite a hiding and
still no victory.

The finish of the race had been moved to another part
of the town new to me as was the very unusual happening of
a strong wind blowing up the valley instead of down. All
my efforts were coming to naught against this wind and,
from 15 miles to go when I was a minute clear my lead disappeared and I was caught and passed by a big group just
three quarters of a mile from the line and I finished well
down! It was a most upsetting experience, I can tell you,
but it was worse when I telephoned Helen. She was staying
over at Australian Reg Arnold's place with his wife Mar-
garet, and they had all watched the event on the 'telly'.
Helen was so sympathetic over the phone I just burst into
tears, which sent her off straightaway for she was on the verge
of them anyhow, and that started the Arnolds off too!

My time must come, I kept telling myself, I had proved
to my own satisfaction that I was good, if not better
than, I had ever been and immediately after putting down
the telephone I asked Gaston Plaud to enter me for Bordeaux–Paris.

# 16

# A New Arrival Brings Luck

THE Bordeaux–Paris classic is more than just a race; it is one of the supreme tests of endurance in cycling. It covers a total distance of 356 miles non-stop with, after 180 miles, a pacing motor taking the rider the rest of the way. Not for nothing is it referred to as the 'Derby of the Road' and it would obviously need tremendous preparation.

The race was to take place at the end of May and so I had about a month in which to get ready. I went home with the knowledge that I was as good now as I had ever been. While at home getting really fit, both mentally and physically, I could also help Helen, as our baby was due in the next few weeks.

I trained hard during my stay and had arranged to leave for Bordeaux by car with my masseur on the Monday afternoon before the event on the following Sunday. This would give me plenty of time to get there and to train a little instead of rushing from one race to the next, as usually happened. On the day before I was due to leave our new arrival had shown no signs of appearing and I was beginning to get a little hot under the collar. I did not want to leave Helen on her own but could not afford to sacrifice this big chance of winning, for I was now convinced that I could win if I stuck to my training schedule.

I just couldn't leave it later than 4 p.m. on the Monday

afternoon and began to feel rather despondent not only at
leaving Helen, but also of not seeing the baby, but things
turned out much better than I expected. At 6 o'clock on
the Monday morning, Helen had me suddenly wide awake
by telling me that the pains had started.

She reckons that I got out of bed quicker than ever before and it is still a record. Talk about panic stations! I did
not know what to do first. I sat there on the edge of the bed
clutching the alarm clock and trying to time the frequency
of the pains. Everything seemed to be going according to
plan and I got the car out at 7 a.m. so that all was ready in
case of a rush, and telephoned the doctor.

He seemed to think there was nothing to worry about and
told me to get Helen down to the hospital by 10 a.m. After
my immediate carryings on this was a bit of an anticlimax,
but I started to pack. I had to get Helen's case ready too and
was flying about the house in a right old state. Eventually,
after a great deal of fussiness I got her to the hospital and by
lunchtime we had another daughter, Joanne. Well, what a
send-off! I was able to see both of them settled and comfort-
able before I left for Bordeaux in a very happy and con-
tented state of mind. Talk about the luck of the devil!

We took things easy on the journey, stopping overnight
en route. We had six days to get to our destination so there
was no need to hurry. I did a little training on the way,
about 60 miles, some of it behind the car. Certainly no more
than that and we arrived at our hotel with a day or so to
spare.

At 1 a.m. on the Sunday morning I signed on in readiness
for the start about an hour later. I felt relaxed and cheerful
despite having fainted in my room about five hours earlier.
What happened I don't know, but I found myself on the
bedroom floor near the washbasin. How long I had been
there I had no idea, but it could not have been for any

great length of time. This had only happened to me once before and that was in the World Championships in 1959 —just before the road race. I was worried about it then and went to see a doctor. He told me it was purely nervous tension and that I had nothing to worry about. Certainly it never affected me then and I felt fine at Bordeaux and realised that I had worked myself up into quite a state.

All signs of nervousness, though, had gone as we started off on our first section of the race—180 miles before picking up the 'dernys', as the pacing-machines are called. It was a steady ride and no-one attempted to do anything foolish as we rode through the last part of the night and then into the dawn. It seemed strange in a way, riding along listening to the dawn chorus and watching it get lighter. It was weird too, to see the streets of the towns and villages almost deserted, although there were a few stalwarts out to see us go by.

Soon after the sun had risen and it was full daylight we reached our pacing motors. From then on it was hell let loose. Everyone seemed to attack at once and so I took my time over things, watching two of the favourites, Dutchmen, De Roo and Post. We were all watching each other like hawks until Post punctured. Immediately the pressure went on and De Roo and I forced the pace at the front.

We raced on and it took Post 26 miles of determined chasing to catch us. I was very glad when he did for we were really flying and I was beginning to feel a bit shattered. There was about 12 of us in that group and, with some 80 miles to go, were 13 minutes behind three riders. My pacer, Ferdnand Wambst, a very experienced man, asked me if I was all right, I just nodded and he launched our attack.

It so happened that Post was taking a feed from his team vehicle at the time and so, as I went away, De Roo tried to hold me. For a few hundred yards he stayed there just a short distance from my back wheel and then, 'pouf!' He blew up and I was alone. For 42 kilometres I chased and then joined the trio which suddenly lost a man as I arrived.

I stayed with them for a time, getting my second wind as it were, while the news of the main field was passed up to me. They were being whipped up to frenzy by Post and De Roo and now trailed by seven minutes. Reaching the 40-miles-to-go-point I realised that my two companions were tired and no longer wanted to work. I had no desire to drag them on to the finish and, spurred on by the information that the main group were now only $1\frac{1}{2}$ minutes behind us, thought it was time to get going. Wambst must have been reading my thoughts for he, almost at the same moment, decided that the bunch had got near enough and steadily put on pressure.

We soon dropped the others and were out alone and in the lead as we went into the Valley of Chevreuse. I felt terrific and told myself that this was it at last. No nerves, no worries and certainly no feeling of tiredness now with victory in sight. Wambst increased the pace a bit as we passed along the road with some 15 miles to go, the crowds packed tight along the route and cheering madly. I was enjoying myself, especially as the news came through that I was over six minutes clear.

As we were passing the Pont de Sevres I spoke to Wambst for the first time in all that distance together. I told him to sprint for the prime at the Parc des Princ. This was for the fastest lap of the track and it meant the completion of a full lap after crossing the finish line inside the stadium. The prize was worth about £75 and I told Wambst that it was to be a present for him from me. He turned slightly in his saddle and I shall always remember what he said. 'No, no, Tom! I'm not sprinting,' he replied. 'You've done quite enough today and I wouldn't ask it of you.'

As we approached the Parc I knew that, at long last, victory was mine. Nothing could stop me now and we entered the stadium to a great roar from the packed stands and terraces. Again I tried to get Wambst to go for the prime but he would not have it. Nevertheless we did a very fast lap and I was out of the saddle and going flat out as we came into the final straight. My time though was beaten by Peter Post by one tenth of a second when he brought in the main group over 11 minutes later. Another Dutchman, Rentmeester, was second just under six minutes behind me.

What joy! What a moment! I was 'proper choked' and had a good old cry right there in the track centre. It was absolutely wonderful and I felt on top of the world. It was two years and a month since I had won a race. In that long spell I had collected second place thirteen times in top events and quite a number of thirds but all these near misses were forgotten in my triumph. After doing the lap of honour I gave my bouquet to M. Hailliez and rushed home to share the fun of it all with Helen. The continental papers carried my victory in headlines that seemed nearly a foot high and, nicest of all, everybody in France and Belgium were delighted about it.

I was a star once more, everyone wanted my autograph and to shake my hand. I enjoyed every minute of it and sharing it with my friends. More important, the promoters remembered me again and a number of good contracts came my way. The only fly in the ointment came when I asked my sponsors, Peugeot, for more money. After all, I was their best rider more or less, admittedly over the last few months —less! But they were not interested and we could not come to terms about my riding in the Tour de France. As I was still not under contract to them and regarded the fee they offered for the Tour too small, I told them I would not ride. There was a lot of talk but we could not agree so I turned to England once more and landed a good contract to ride in the Isle of Man professional event. Naturally I was pleased to be back in Britain and was anxious to ride well in front of my old friends and supporters.

It turned out to be a very hard race because of terrible weather conditions. It poured with rain and there were great gusts of wind up to 80 m.p.h. which certainly did not help on the big climbs over the mountain. Naturally the home-based independents wanted to do well and things were fairly tight on the first few laps. Eventually Zilverberg had gone away on his own and the 74 starters were beginning to dwindle.

I decided that it was time to go in those last few laps and launched an attack. I went clear with Frenchman Hamon and the Spaniard Manzano. Hamon was willing to work but not so Manzano. He stuck behind us all the way up the Dutchman and I got very cross about it. I knew him pretty well and recalled that he had a good sprint. I never mind being beaten by a man who has done his share of the work but the 'wheel-sucker' always make me angry.

As we were riding along I went back to him and said, 'If we come to a sprint and you bloody beat me you'll never put your leg over another bike. I'll flatten you, boy!' I think the message got home but it had no immediate effect for he never moved to the front. Anyway I went ahead on a descent where there was a bad bend and stayed clear to win alone. Whether Manzano hadn't the strength to get up to me or whether he decided that discretion was the better part of valour, I shall never know. He won the sprint for second place but there were only fourteen other finishers, which gives an indication of how hard it was.

I returned to Ghent just about the time the Tour de France began. I had decided to have a rest before preparing for the 'Worlds' and so left my bike alone for a bit. Helen's parents came over, primarily to see their new grand-daughter of course, and I took my father-in-law out to see a little of the Tour, while it was in Belgium.

Time passed quickly as it was pleasant having them over, but my three weeks' rest proved to be a big mistake. By the time the after-Tour criteriums began I was as slow as a tortoise and suffered quite a lot in the early events. All the other riders were well 'run in' and I took some hammerings in those races, I can tell you.

About a fortnight before the 'Worlds' which, incidentally, were being held in Belgium, I had a series of accidents which did not help matters. They all took place in less than a week and the effect was far worse than if they had been over a longer period. First my forks broke when cornering and I took quite a tumble. Then I blew a tyre on a sharp bend and fell heavily again. I can't for the life of me remember how the third one occurred but I know I felt pretty groggy after it.

I suppose there must have been a build-up of shock as a result of these falls for I went through a really bad patch. I lost about 10 lbs in 36 hours, was passing blood and felt terribly ill for about three days, but the doctor soon had me to rights and within a week I was feeling well again.

Despite being a little weak I felt pretty good when the time came to start the World Championship Road Race. I didn't think the illness had done me any harm but, one never knows really and it may have affected me. The race was at Renaix and around a tough twelve mile circuit. I think there were 14 laps to be covered and before the start I asked Ramsbottom and the other British lads if they would ride for me. 'Rams' said he wanted to have a go himself, Denson was ready to 'have a go' but the others were a bit cagey. I was prepared to pay them for their work in much the same way that Van Looy had done to gain his own two titles. Whether they didn't believe me or just weren't interested I don't know so I tried to get the other two English speaking riders, Irishmen Shay Elliot and Peter Crinnion, on my side too, hoping that we could all 'gang up' against the continentals and give them a taste of their own medicine.

So the race began. The Belgians blocked everything because Van Looy was again offering his team mates good money if they helped him to victory. 50,000 Belgian francs or £350 per man was the price he offered and, one way or another, they managed to ruin the whole race. With only about three laps to the finish I managed to get away with Elliott. He worked a bit at the front and I said to him, 'Come on then, Sam, we've got to work if we're going to win, one of us.' He was noncommittal about it and I had the feeling that he was only there to mark me. I offered him the same price that Van Looy was giving his team but he told me it wasn't enough. I doubled it in desperation, for I did so want to win and especially to beat the Belgian combine. All this time he was working a bit but his heart was not in it. Eventually he said, 'I can't do it, Tom, after all I don't ride for Peugeot.' I knew what he meant and realised that there would be a lot of angry men in his own team if he helped me.

It might have affected his contract for the following year and I certainly did not blame him for refusing to help. So, with just about a lap to go we were caught by a bunch of 26 riders. Everyone stayed together and, as we took the last corner into the finishing straight, about 400 yards from the line, Frenchman Guy Ignolin was just in the lead.

His sprint was too early and he 'died' about 200 yards from the finish and I went past him. A number of men came up alongside me now, all of us going like the clappers. I would not have won, as there were a number of much better sprinters around me but then, bang! Van Looy grabbed me by the jersey and just about brought me to a standstill!

I managed to get going again, now in the middle of the bunch when, hell's bells! Dutchman Jan Janssens gave me a whacking great pull and just about stopped me completely. I should have gone up and given him a good thump round the earhole but what was the use? I did not see the finish for, by now I was right at the back and, in fact, was placed 28th, last man in the sprint. It was not a finish that anyone would really want to witness from what I heard and read about afterwards, for it was a complete fiasco.

As we all came towards the finish Van Looy was shouting desperately for someone to give him a wheel to pace him to the front. He asked Benoni Beheyt but was told he had cramp. He did get another Belgian to tow him along but not fast enough and so he pulled me to gain himself some extra impetus. Beheyt was foxing and, taking the inside, had gone to the front under his own power. As I was told, Van Looy saw him and switched across the road trying to ward him off. Just about side by side, Beheyt got hold of Van Looy's jersey and I reckon must have said to himself, 'Should I push him? Should I hell!' And so he pulled him as his captain was trying to push him away and took the title by inches. A perfect example of the biter being bitten.

# 17

# A Trip to the Pacific

IN MANY ways it was not a championship to remember but I was soon back to good form again. We won the Grand Prix Parisienne team time trial which put all the Peugeot riders in a very happy frame of mind. I was now in second place in the Super-Prestige-Pernod Trophy behind Anquetil and one point ahead of Poulidor.

This trophy probably means very little outside cycling circles, but for those involved it is very important. Points are awarded for various events throughout the season according to one's placing and it is rather like an unofficial world championship. Equally important, there were cash prizes too and I was determined that Poulidor was not going to get ahead of me.

After the time trial event I won a few criteriums and then we came to the classic Paris–Tours event. It was a terrible day, with wind and rain, and it was bitterly cold too. Not long after the start I punctured and got the surprise of my life. The whole Peugeot team came straight off the back to assist me! We were a team of aces in a way and were certainly not renowned for team work up to that time.

Anyhow there they were, all ready to pace me back into the race. It was fabulous really and it had a tremendous effect on me. It made me feel great, terrific in fact, and in a very short time, whoosh! I was back in the field. I thought to myself, Blimey! I must do something now to show them just how grateful I am but, as the race wore on the weather got worse and it began to get me down.

So much so, in fact, that I half considered packing it in, but I wasn't going to do that if Poulidor stayed there because I had no intention of handing over my lead in the trophy to him. So, as we plodded along the road I said to him, 'Do you feel like abandoning, Raymond?' But no, he would not come across so I decided then and there that I would beat him.

I forget how the attack came about. It was just one of those things that suddenly happen in a race and it is difficult to recall, even immediately afterwards, the circumstances that lead up to a break going away. I do recall, however, that shortly before the attack I crashed when I hit a wall after skidding on the wet road as I crossed a bridge. The roads were very wet and greasy and there were riders piling up all over the place. At one point a car braked and skidded into the bunch, knocking down a number of men. My fall was nothing serious. I did not hurt myself at all and was on the field in no time.

The break came just as I had caught up and I was with it. We were only a small group and it included Poulidor but, as we came up for the sprint, the Dutchman De Roo went clear to get the decision by about a length and a half with Poulidor and myself fighting for second place. It was a very close affair and a photofinish. At first they gave it to the Frenchman but the picture showed that I had got second place by about two inches, so Poulidor was placed third and that placing earned me another ten points towards the Super-Prestige-Pernod Trophy.

Then came the Tour of Lombardy where again I kept a close watch on Poulidor. He never went anywhere without having me on his wheel, for I marked him like you would mark a piece of wood with paint. He went to the wall with nerves eventually, just cracking all of a sudden, and so I did not have to worry about guarding my position for the trophy. Perhaps because I was so busy keeping an eye on Raymond I missed the break but had some satisfaction from winning the sprint in the big bunch finish to take 10th place.

After that a rest and a few thoughts about riding the indoor Sixes. I got the chance of riding the Brussels Six but then something almost out of this world came up which made me cancel the offer.

Along with a number of other riders I was invited to race in New Caledonia, an island very rich in nickel in the Pacific about 1,000 miles from Australia. About 46,000 Europeans lived there and a number of big business men among them combined to arrange a number of meetings. Naturally I jumped at the chance of going and left about the middle of November with Anquetil, Anglade, Christoff, Baldini, Elliott and De Roo. Stablinski should have come with us but he had been involved in a bad accident and so the poor chap had to stay behind.

What a fabulous place it is and what a wonderful time we had! The weather was gorgeous and we were all out swimming every day. I went fishing, spear fishing as well as by line, and also hunted giant turtles. The natives were marvellous at skin diving and some of them could go down about 40 or 50 feet without breathing apparatus.

We visited a real desert island one day, the 'Island of Pines' it was called, and I became as brown as a berry. The food was terrific and we stayed at an enormous ranch all the time we were there. One dish I shall always remember was a special thing done with raw fish. I don't know what sort of fish it was but it was chopped up and then left to soak in lemon juice for a long time. Then it was mixed with fresh coconut and served with rice and salad. It was grand, but I don't think it would work with cod!

Fruit too was so plentiful, pineapple, even lychees were fresh and, although we raced hard there—I expect you were wondering when I was going to do some work!—it was almost a holiday. I found out more about Anquetil during our stay than I would ever have done in France. He became a real person there, alive and friendly, not a bit like the cold, calculating rider that everyone knows in his own country. He really was, away from the French public and his fans, excellent company and an extremely nice man.

In a way I was sorry to leave for it was the most wonderful place and I am determined that, one day, I shall go there again. I brought a lot of souvenirs home, including a giant turtle shell, and arrived back in time to spend Christmas in England. I felt on top of the world, fit, happy and well rested and was looking forward to doing some great things in the new year.

Instead of going south as I usually did in January, I took Helen and the family up to the French Alps for about a month. We rented a chalet in St. Gervais and had a grand time. We went because most of the top riders went there every winter and since I was 'one of the boys' now I had to show my face in the right places, for publicity purposes if nothing else.

There wasn't much skiing to be done for there was little snow around, but the weather was great and that was all that mattered. They hold the Cyclists' Ski Championship in the area and there is always a good 'do' afterwards. We were invited to this and I remember asking the organiser if it would be necessary to wear suit and tie etc., or if the ordinary 'après ski' wear was OK. He said that sweaters and slacks would be fine, so we turned up that way to find the majority clad in their Sunday suits!

It didn't matter much for everybody knew everybody else and the champagne was soon flowing. Now I'm not a drinking man at all, an odd glass of ale now and again when I'm home and, occasionally a glass of wine, but rarely any more. That was the night I found out that champagne was very potent—for me anyhow! Two glasses and I was ready for anything and anything meant me snipping off the ties of the male guests.

It must have been a laugh, not that I remember much of it, for when I got home Helen found the ends of 16 ties in my pockets! Probably the biggest laugh was when I cut part of Gaston Plaud's tie off. I had, of course, now signed a contract for Peugeot and, accordingly, he was my big boss. As I said, my memory about that night is very hazy but I certainly remember Plaud leaning over our table with his tie spilling out from under his jacket.

What a challenge! Well, I could not resist that and very quickly had my scissors out and, snip! One section of the tie was in my hand and under the table. The biggest laugh came when he thought I hadn't got him and waved the other, remaining, part of the tie good-naturedly at me. His face when I brought the other piece out and dangled it in front of him was a study! His wife laughed loudest of all, and, I think, saved the day for me!

All good things come to an end sometime and, at the end of the month, I departed for the south to prepare myself for the coming battles. Although I had been off the bike for a time I was still quite fit and it did not take long for me to hit good form.

The first event was, as usual, Paris–Nice in which I wanted to ride my own way and use each stage as a special training ride in readiness for the Milan–San Remo. I was set on winning it and knew that if I carefully rode myself in, it could be mine without a lot of difficulty.

So, along the road to Nice, I took things fairly steadily, having a go now and then and feeling better and better as the time went on. On the final stage, which went out on a loop over the mountains from Nice and back again, I decided to give myself a short, sharp session and then retire. The consequences of this were to come up again at a later date, but the immediate repercussions were loud, long and unprintable!

I hadn't got a lot of miles in my legs when I started, unlike some of the riders, and so thought that a few fast rides over short distances would do me just as well. I had been offered a ride in the Antwerp Six but since they were not prepared to pay my price I didn't go. I was still remembering the advice from George Berger and Cyril Cartwright about 'cheapening' myself and, in recent years this wisdom had been backed by my French Agent, Daniel Dousset.

I had ridden strongly in the mountains in Corsica in the previous stages and, after a short warm-up along the Promenade des Anglais in Nice, was ready for a flyer at the start. Beginning from the flat the race immediately rises up the big climb of La Turbie, up on to the Grand Corniche and then down into Monaco. I thought to myself, 'I'll stir things up here' and boom! I was off straightaway up the climb, stringing the field out like elastic. Riders were going off right and left such was the speed I put on as we ascended. Altig came after me, defending his colleague Anquetil who had the jersey and caught me halfway up. He was furious like a lot of others but I wasn't finished yet! As soon as he reached me I attacked again and went away. Once more I was caught and still I attacked and broke clear. By now the field were in ribbons, the whole Philco team had retired and everybody hated my guts but I just did not care.

I was riding to my plan to win Milan–San Remo and reckoned this was the best way of doing it! Hard luck on the others, I thought, and had a bit of a laugh to myself about it, little realising as I said before that my 'preparation' was to backfire on me later in the year. At the top of La Turbie I had a reasonable lead and so coasted down towards Monaco, eventually stopping at the roadside. I had had a good sweat and used little or no energy and stood there grinning as the riders went by. I just waved to them, said 'Ciou!' and rode back to Nice via the coast road. There I changed happily, having done only about 40 of the 180 kilometres of the stage, and departed for Italy.

So to the Milan–San Remo 1964, the 288 kilometre Italian classic. The first event was run back in 1907 when the great French rider, Petit-Breton, won it. I was determined, as a Great Briton, to win the 55th race but knew that I had felt this way many times before in my career. But on 19th March as we formed up for the start I had the feeling inside me that the race was in my pocket.

Two hundred and thirty-two professionals moved off on that long ride but, by the time we reached the Capa Berta climb, with 25 miles to go, there were only four of us. It happened quite quickly, that getaway from the big group, and was started by an Italian rider just before we began the ascent. George Van Conningsloo, one of my team mates, went away with him and then moved across to the left hand side of the road. I was coming up and just pushed past him, using my arm to move him aside. He said afterwards that I pushed him back into the bunch, and I suppose I may have done, but it was not intentional.

Poulidor was on my wheel and hung there like a leech as I pulled away. The Belgian, Willy Bocklandt, came with us too and in a matter of a few hundred yards we were clear. I went like the devil up the climb, towing the others all the way. Over the top and I began to descend like the clappers! Once on the flat the other three worked as well and I became a bit worried about Bocklandt for he had a terrific sprint.

We were all clear now and as it turned out I need not have worried about the Belgian. On the last climb, the Poggio, Poulidor attacked very strongly and I went with him leaving the other two on the lower slopes. The Frenchman was about 5 or 10 yards in the lead, really hammering along and I decided to pull him back steadily and not overwork myself. As soon as I got his wheel he went again, whoosh! Once more he was clear by about ten yards and, gradually, I joined up with him. Three of four times he tried this and each time I slowly hauled him back. I wasn't making the violent efforts that he was and felt full of fight as we reached the summit together

We came down fast, Poulidor now quite unable to drop me on the descent. As we levelled out with only about a kilometre to go I took the lead. I reckoned that with someone like Poulidor it was best to lead him out but still have something under my foot—something in reserve. I started my sprint about 500 yards from the line, out of the saddle and pushing quite a big gear, 53 × 14 for the enthusiasts! Along the finishing stretch of road, the Via Roma, there is a slight rise, nothing much, hardly more than a few feet in about 200 yards, but this may have affected him. Anyhow I began to accelerate but saw him come up alongside me.

I put on a bit more pressure and he came again. He still tried to get at my side and didn't seem to have the tactical sense of getting on my wheel, thereby forcing me to pull him along. So, as he went faster, I kept accelerating and that was that! I was over the line well clear for my third classic victory.

The papers gave the result a great show and I rushed home to share my triumph with Helen and the family. When I arrived the house was full of flowers, telegrams were

arriving from all over the Continent, the phone kept ringing
—it was wonderful bedlam !

I was invited out to a reception in Ghent, at my friend
Albert's café, and what a surprise was waiting for Helen and
I when we got there ! The local band from St. Amandsberg
were outside in full force to honour me and, I'll never really
know why, played 'It's A Long Way To Tipperary.'
Whether they thought it was the British national anthem
or whether they could not play 'God Save The Queen' re-
mains a mystery, but it was grand of them to do such a thing.
After all, what does it matter if the thought is there?

We were given a smashing time. Albert's mother, 'Ma'
as she is affectionately known to me and many other young
British riders, had laid on a marvelous reception. We thoroughly enjoyed ourselves and, once more, I realised the importance of winning a classic.

# 18

# Frayed Tempers

SOON, I was on the move again, going South towards the Côte d'Azur for the three-day Tour du Var. I was still in very good form and won the first stage, thereby taking over the leader's jersey. The next day, stage two, saw little excitement at first and I managed to watch and control all the moves that went on at the front.

Everything was going according to plan until about 3 miles from the finish when we arrived in a village. There, right before my eyes was a frightening great hill! When I had looked on the map before starting the stage I had not realised that the route wound back over the village behind St. Tropez where we finished.

Immediately Anquetil attacked and broke away, taking Frenchman Henri Anglade with him. That was that! I couldn't get near them at all and Anquetil won the stage and Anglade took over the leadership. When I finished, a little way behind them, I thought 'You rotten boggers.' I was very cross with Anquetil in particular for he has always been against Anglade and they are reputed to be arch-enemies.

I taxed him about this afterwards and he just smiled his quiet smile and said, 'The penny has two faces, you know, Tom. Good deeds are always repaid and bad ones too.' I did not understand him at all and asked him what I had done to incur his disfavour. He smiled again. 'Do you remember the last stage in Paris–Nice?' he asked, and suddenly, click, and I knew! 'You would never have lost this race,' he went on, 'if you hadn't played around and made a monkey out of everyone on that last day.'

Right at that moment I realised that I was still learning and I wasn't as clever as I had thought. He taught me that one needs friends in cycling probably more than in any other sport and I was, and still am, grateful to him for the lesson—hard though it was. The incident is forgotten now. I like to regard him as a friend, despite our battles on the bike, and I am privileged to have had the opportunity of racing against him—and sometimes beating him! But it was a lesson I never forgot.

I rode all the classics, apart from Bordeaux–Paris, and rode quite well without doing anything spectacular. It seemed now that I was more content to take things as they came. After all, I had now won three classics and was a 'name' in the continental cycling sphere. There was no further need for me to try hard all the time and I was now sufficiently mature to have lost a little of my impulsiveness.

My immediate sights were on the Tour de France. I held no big ideas of winning, much as I wanted to, for Anquetil was riding and, apart from his tremendous ability he had terrific team backing. I would be quite happy in finishing in the first five and reckoned this was far from impossible.

Before starting the tour, I went over to the Isle of Man and rode the 'pro' event. I knew that the British independents were out for my blood and would do their utmost to beat me. This was fairly obvious and the other riders that came over with me realised they could profit from it, as I would be the marked man.

When a group containing nearly all the continental riders

got clear without me the British riders sat on me. They were
waiting for me to take them up and only Bill Holmes was
intelligent enough to ride his own race and ignore me. I just
sat there happily and, when I eventually made my attack,
it was too late to catch the leaders. The race was won by
Shay Elliott and I thought the home based men would have
been taught a lesson in tactics. I was wrong though, as I was
to learn later.

No sooner was I back on the other side of the Channel
than it was the start of the Tour and I immediately
began on the wrong foot! Right at the start, as we were all
waiting to move off on the first stage I had a dust-up with
Anglade.

It was silly, really, now I look back on it, for it was only
gossip that began it all. Alan Ramsbottom was the innocent
cause of the argument for the tongues had wagged about
him after he was not chosen for the Tour with other members of the Pelforth team. I had got 'Rams' fixed up in Belgium as we were friends off the bike, but he had never ridden
for me nor I for him. It had been said that he would help
me in the Tour and so, because of these silly rumours, he
was out of the race, or so it seemed anyway.

Anglade, as a senior member of the Pelforth squad,
might, I thought, have had some say in this and so I tackled
him about it. 'You're a fine fellow,' I said to him. 'Poor old
Ramsbottom's not in the Tour. It doesn't matter to you
that he relies on races like this for his living.' 'Oh!' said
Anglade. 'What's it got to do with you? Are you upset because you've lost a team mate?'

The words flew back and forth. It was all a lot of hot air
on both sides but the heat of it was beginning to build up
inside me! By now our raised voices had attracted quite a
number of journalists plus some riders. The row went on and
I found myself getting so annoyed that I was losing my now

very good command of the French language. So I thought
I won't talk any more, I'll just thump him!

I made a grab at his jersey to pull him on to a 'fourpenny
one' but I was grabbed instead. The Press men and some
riders, I have no idea who they were or how many, kept me
away from the Frenchman and so I sat there boiling and
muttering until the start. Once we were off I chased Anglade
and got on his wheel. Where he went I went, the Tour was
of secondary importance. The pair of us played silly devils
like that for the whole stage and might have carried on the
squabble had it not been for some impartial intervention.
This came from René De Latour who got us together before
the second day's start and made us shake hands. That broke
the spell and I'm glad it did for I have always liked and respected Henri.

With the altercation settled I took the Tour seriously as
was essential if I was to do a good ride. Things went
smoothly enough for me in those first ten days and I went
well enough on the first real Alpine stage. This was from
Thonon-les-Bains to Briançon which takes in two big
climbs. These were the Col du Télégraphe, which is really
a stepping stone to the giant Galibier, soaring up 8,400 feet
into the snow piled at the roadside.

I was going well on this stage although I was nowhere
near the great climber, Bahamontes of Spain, better known
as the 'Eagle of Toledo', who went away on his own. But on
the long 20 miles run down into Briançon I met up with bad
luck; I punctured. I wasn't in the lead but not far off and
my ability to descend fast could possibly have given me second place behind the 'Eagle' and a 30 second time bonus. As
it was I lost 1½ minutes because my team car with the spares
was such a long time coming. I was very annoyed about this
and the incident shook some of my confidence in Gaston
Plaud and the members of the Peugeot team.

The next day we headed south to Monaco, again with two big climbs, the Col de Vars and the mighty Restefond. It was a hot day but I stuck to my guns and kept with the leaders. Once over the Vars we descended until the beginning of the colossal climb of the Restefond. It towered ahead of us with its tiny, winding road taking us up and up and up. It seems as though you are climbing into the clouds for it is a big one—over 9,000 feet above sea level.

On the descent to Monaco, two small groups merged. I was with them and hoped to gain the winner's one minute bonus from the other 21 men when we reached the cinder track in Monte Carlo. As is usual in stadium finishes, you come in, cross the line and then complete a lap to finish. For some unknown reason Poulidor, who was just in front of me as we entered the stadium, as was Anquetil, went for the sprint. Naturally, as he eased after crossing the line, Anquetil and I passed him and went like the clappers round the track. Cinders are not easy to sprint on and Jacques had the advantage of being in the lead. I could not get round him and had to be content with second.

Next day we moved along the Mediterranean coast to Hyères. The temperature was about 90 degrees in the shade and no one hurried in the early part of the stage! It is traditional anyway for the Tour to have a bit of a 'promenade' along this stretch, nine days racing and the Alps behind, who could blame us? I longed to stir things up a bit just for a laugh but knew I must contain myself. For, apart from remembering the lesson that Anquetil had taught me, there were two stages that day. After the finish at Hyères we had an individual time trial stage of 13 miles.

I wanted to do well in that but somehow or other I just couldn't get going at all and took 20th place. Not surprisingly Anquetil won it and moved into second place overall behind little George Groussard.

Two more days and we were in the tiny country of Andorra, high in the Pyrenees. We had a rest day there and I took stock of things. I was still in the fight, holding 10th place overall, less than 5½ minutes behind Groussard. There was a lot of tough climbing to come for the Pyrenees were by no means over yet, but I felt quite pleased with the situation.

Then things went haywire. I suppose the earlier happenings hadn't been too good, losing my temper at the start and then having the upset of the puncture and no team car. Both instances had put me out of my normal good humour and it is surprising how silly little things like that can affect my performance.

What was to come failed to help matters. I had tried to telephone Helen from Andorra without success. There seemed to be no more than a couple of telephones in the whole country and you can imagine what it is like there when about 70 journalists descend upon the place! I could not get through to her. She wasn't at home as the Tour people had asked her to join Mesdames Anquetil and Stablinski for a publicity campaign that was going on ahead of the race. We had left the children with friends and I had arranged to 'phone her from Andorra.

Late that night I got a telegram which just said 'Telephone. Very urgent. Helen'. Well I became worried but I could not get through no matter where I tried. Next morning, as we prepared for the ride to Toulouse, another telegram arrived. It was much the same as before. 'Telephone. Very, very urgent. Helen'.

That really got me going and I was almost beside myself with worry. I went to the Post Office and booked a call straightaway. Difficulties then came up along the lines and there was a delay. I was going back towards the start when a shout took me galloping back. False alarm! Back and forth

I wavered between Post Office and start and, eventually, the race won.

Riders and journalists knew all about my worry for there are few secrets in the Tour and all were sympathetic. It did not help things. People were slapping me on the back and saying, 'It's nothing to worry about. Everyone's all right. Just a mistake' and so on. For me it grew out of all proportion and, by the time the race began, I was in tears. The very least that could have happened was that the children had been killed in an accident or that Helen had been knocked down. All sorts of horrible thoughts entered my head as we moved off along the road.

Halfway up the first hill as I was forcing the pace at the front, one of the 'Tour Radio' cars came up to tell me that they had been in contact with Helen and everything was fine. She had been worried about me because I had not phoned! It was terrific of them to have gone to all that trouble and I think Plaud was at the back of it. Nice of him, too, but he upset me terribly a bit further on. The good news calmed me down so much that I lost all my momentum and, for a short time, went off the back!

I soon returned to the fight and then, on the descent of the Envalira climb, made difficult because of mist, I punctured once more. As before there was no team car. I was furious! I had been fairly well placed but now I stood, fuming at the roadside watching riders go past me. Team cars came down but not mine and then, to add insult to injury, Anquetil went past and I had been a minute clear of him at the top of the climb!

Eventually I got a wheel from Mastrotto, one of my team mates, but the damage was done. I had lost $2\frac{1}{2}$ minutes and, what was worse still, had lost all faith in Peugeot and Plaud. I had felt nearly all through the race that I wasn't getting the attention I deserved. This was bad for my morale especially as I was the leading Peugeot rider.

The incident seemed to crown a host of silly little things that I would never have mentioned otherwise and I was absolutely livid about the whole affair. With my calmness gone again I was erratic and fed up and decided that to do anything I had to fight against Peugeot, my own bad luck and all the other riders as well!

We rode on. Toulouse to Luchon where I tried hard to pull back some of my lost time but failed. I did not have the strength that I normally have and, when the heat was really on, I could not respond. I had not dropped behind but I felt that when I called for that extra effort it just was not there.

That night I did not feel too well. I was with some friends at dinner and suddenly had to get up and excuse myself. It was not like me and I recalled that a number of riders had suffered from sickness in this area on previous Tours. There had been a few complaints about food in some of the stage towns and I hoped that I would be all right next day.

This was to be the big ride for it was the stage of the 'Four Cols.' This was, perhaps, the hardest day of all and one where you could gain a lot and lose much more. I lost, and badly too. The four big climbs are legend in the Tour history, the Peyresourde, Aspin, Tourmalet and the Aubisque. Things began well for I took the first mountain quite easily with the leaders. On the Aspin I found my strength ebbing and slowly but surely I dropped back. Desperately I tried to fight my way on. Descending very fast I caught up with them and then, crack! Off I went once more on the Tourmalet. I watched the field go past, pedalling slowly and grimly on. I was well down as I went over the summit and there was still the Aubisque to come.

I thought I would never get to Pau and suffered agonies on that last climb. I made it but lost nearly 20 minutes and that was the finish for me. Strangely enough I felt better the next day, and in fact rode well for the rest of the race. How frustrating life can get! So at Paris I was way, way down in 14th place, some ten positions further back than I had intended to be. Disheartened, tired and very much out of humour I prepared for the usual run of criterium events that follow the Tour.

Coming home from one of these about two days after Paris I stopped the car to go to the toilet. I found out then the possible reasons for my ups and downs in the Tour. I had a tape-worm. I was horrified and felt unclean. I knew that Anquetil had ridden with one some time ago and it had not bothered him, but it seemed awful to me to have such a thing.

I thought I had better get rid of it but some people suggested I kept it until after the World Championship in September. They argued that the necessary treatment might make me too ill to ride in the title race or, if I did, the after-effects would slow me down.

As I mentioned I felt awful about it but felt there might be something in their argument so I ignored it as much as possible and tried not thinking about it.

I had signed a contract to ride in London at the end of July on the Crystal Palace circuit and was looking forward to it. It was a Sunday race over 50 miles only and Elliott, Ramsbottom and a few others came over with me. This was where the British riders learned another lesson, not to let a break get too far away, even early on. It was a hard circuit with a sharp little climb on each lap. As we started the second lap I went away with Rams and Elliott and two British based riders. We shook them off in a lap or so and then rode on.

Why they did not chase us then I shall never know, but they just sat there and watched us go away. There was a very good crowd there, about 12,000, and they roared their disapproval of the negative riding from the bunch. Once again Billy Holmes was the only one to show some real fight and he, together with George Van Conningsloo, were the only men that failed to get lapped!

The sprint finish was chaos as we were all mixed up with the bunch, having caught them a few laps earlier, but I won with about a length from Elliott with Rams in third place. I really enjoyed being back in England again and finding such a large and appreciative audience.

It was only a day trip, unfortunately, and I was soon back in the criteriums in France and Belgium. The tapeworm was beginning to get on my mind now and, with only ten days left to the 'Worlds', I decided to get rid of it. I just could not stand the thought of it any longer, took the necessary poison and away it went.

# 19

# Ups and Downs

I HAD, in my own way, prepared myself for the World Championship. Through various events I paced myself along, varying my efforts and speeds. The event was being held at Sallanches, a small town in the French Alps, almost at the foot of Mont Blanc.

I felt no serious after-effects of the treatment for killing the tape-worm but looked forward to my sixth bid for the title. I reckoned that I stood a very good chance of success for I was not one of the favourites which, in itself, suited me very well. I kept out of the limelight when I arrived there a few days before the race, staying in a small hotel on the road to Megève a few miles from Sallanches.

I had brought my *soigneur* and, from my hideaway, trained and rested. By the time the big day came I felt very good and brimful of confidence that I would do a good ride. I had told myself that I was going to win and, day after day, had drummed it into my brain. Nothing, I thought, will stop me now. I have had more than my share of bad luck and it's time for a change.

The circuit was not a very difficult one and measured about seven and a quarter miles round. The total distance to be covered was about 174 miles, split up into 24 laps and it was raining! The locals reckoned that it never rained in the area during that time of the year and, in fact, right up

to the Saturday, the sun had shone. It rained all day Saturday and dampened the ardour of both the women's and
the men's amateur title races, and continued on throughout
the Sunday.

There was only one climb, quite a stiff one of about three
miles up to the village of Passy. Then followed a terrifically
fast descent with some sharp corners and here, on the third
lap, I came to grief. I was coming down with the Spaniard
Otano and Italian Taccone and were just clear of the main
field when Otano skidded on the bend. My immediate reaction was to brake, a dangerous thing on the wet road, and
Taccone did the same thing. All three of us shot across the
road virtually on our backsides. I managed to remain on
the roadway, coming to a sudden stop when I hit the bar-
riers at the roadside. I think the others went over the top,
but luckily they weren't much damaged and we were soon
on again. I had torn a piece out of my shorts together
with a piece of flesh from my hip. There were one or
two other lumps and bumps but the important thing was
that the bike was undamaged except for a slightly bent
pedal.

A few laps later a break went with Anglade making the
move to the front. There were six of them and Taccone, who
had come off with me, was up with it. Back in the bunch
nobody bothered very much about it and there was the old
school of Belgians, including Van Looy, taking it easy. The
race wore on and we passed the halfway mark with the
break about six minutes clear.

I thought to myself that it was about time I got going or
I would miss the boat. Coming down the hill from Passy I
was clear with Van Looy, who also descended very fast. We
had opened up quite a sizeable gap as we reached the flat and
I figured that we could get them if he worked with me. I
looked round for him and he had sat up! Obviously he did

not want to work too hard and was waiting for the bunch. I continued my effort and went away.

There were just over nine laps left and I got down 'over the hooks' and kept turning a big gear. Always for the championship I fit a slightly bigger gear—54 × 14 for the technically minded. Gradually I pulled them back but it was hard work with no-one there to help at the front.

Slowly but surely I got nearer. Unfortunately, as I did, the break began to fall apart. When I reached them after 42 miles of chasing, only Anglade and his compatriot, Foucher, remained. There were now less than three laps to go and, as we took the climb up to the village, Foucher departed.

The bunch, now sensing danger, had whipped up to a very fast pace behind us and were closing rapidly. Poor Anglade had nothing left and I was beginning to tire. As we came to the climb for the last time but one, Adorni and Janssens got up to us. Straightaway, Adorni attacked up the hill. I could have wept! I threshed away at the pedals to keep them with me but lost ground. I caught them on the descent and we rode through together for the final lap. The rest of the bunch were now nearly with us and Poulidor got on as we came to the climb.

Anglade had dropped back now and that hill was sheer torture. I was getting cramp in my leg too, whether it was because of the bent pedal or the rain or perhaps a combination of both, I just do not know, but it hurt! Taking a quick look over my shoulder as we climbed, I saw the others strung out behind.

My strength was going fast and I don't know how I kept clear of them all. The other three had dropped me as I reached the top, but again I came back at them on the way down. This was it, now or never, and I tried and tried to get on terms. Into the right-hander about 300 yards from the line and they were all a matter of a few lengths in front of me. Could I find enough to take me past them? No. I could not even find enough strength to get up to them!

I was dead and I could not lie down. I watched miserably as Janssens took it from Adorni with Poulidor just behind, and myself bringing up the rear for fourth place. Fourth again and I was a very disappointed man. I had given everything I had and was nowhere. It was a big effort and I knew I had really taken it out of myself. Disappointed was not the word. I was shattered both mentally and physically and the kind things said about me in the continental press were of no use at all.

They said I was the moral victor but there were no crumbs of comfort in that and certainly no money for my wife and family. I had ridden to win and failed. Failed as I had done so many times before. When, I wondered, will I make it?

No peace for the wicked, they say, and it was not long before I was riding Paris–Tours. I had no intention of winning for I had set my sights on the Tour of Lombardy and just used the French classic as a training ride. I had won the first and now I wanted to win the last classic of the season.

At Milan I told Gaston Plaud what I wanted in my feed. Just a bottle of water, a bottle of soft drink and no meat sandwiches, but blow me down if, when I received the musette, there was nothing there I wanted. He had put in a bottle of coffee and I hate coffee when I am riding. I just cannot drink it. It comes straight back as I just cannot digest it. I was furious and threw it away in disgust.

I attacked on the descent of the Gizalo and got away with a group of riders. We went round Lake Maggiore and, on the next climb, I attacked again and soon there were only five of us at the front. On the next col it was the young Italian, Gianni Motta, who attacked and I was the only one to stay with him.

We were clear, just the two of us, with about 50 miles to go but, of course, I had no food. I had eaten everything in my pockets at the start and had thrown away the replenishments that Plaud had given me. Motta very kindly gave me a bidon of mashed up fruit which helped me over a bit but it was not very sustaining. Then, on the last climb but one before the finish, we received the news that a group were chasing at 50 seconds. Poulidor, Adorni, Janssens and a whole band of them.

So I thought, well, they're not going to get us back and I really hammered away on that climb. Motta hardly ever passed me and at the summit we had about three minutes lead. But I had just about shot my bolt I think as, on the descent, I began to feel very tired. As we hit the flat by the lake going towards Como I felt shattered. I knew it was lack of food and, at the time, I blamed Plaud completely for this. Looking back, I realise that everybody makes mistakes sometimes. Nonetheless this hurt me awfully and I could not understand why he did not seem to care about me.

Along that stretch of road it really began to hurt and I took a real bending. Motta dropped me about 10 miles from the finish for by now I could not even see straight and was riding on my will-power alone. About 20 riders passed me but I hardly remember seeing them go by. I don't even recall going over the final climb, I was just about out on my feet. I must have got over it all right because I finished! I was way down though and young Motta won it.

I went back home feeling tired and very despondent. I was fed up with the road and was looking forward to a rest and then a few indoor Sixes. I rode the Brussels Six in November, partnered by Freddy Eugen the Danish rider. We had a good time with plenty of amusement and finished fourth. Next it was the Zürich Six, this time with Australian Ron Baensch and we had a great time. I really enjoyed myself with a bit of clowning and looked forward to Christmas in England.

After a very happy Christmas and New Year with our families, Helen and I, plus the children, went off once more to our ski chalet for a month's holiday. There was a lot more snow than in 1964 and we all set out to have a great time. For a fortnight everything was fine and then I broke my ankle! It was a silly accident really, being on the last run down the slope for the day. I fell and crack! That was that. Helen was very cut up when I was brought to her, trussed up like a chicken, on a sledge. She had been waiting dinner for me at a local restaurant with some friends and the ski instructor fetched her out to me. Later she said that when she got outside all she could see was a nose sticking out of a mass of straps and bandages!

That ruined the rest of the holiday. I had my ankle in plaster and was a bit worried for I had two contracts for indoor meetings—one of them being the Milan Six, in only a fortnight's time. Luckily it was only a hairline fracture, not too serious, and in twelve days the plaster was taken off.

On the Saturday before the Milan Six began I rode at Antwerp in the European Championship behind the dernys. I got through my heat OK but retired in the final as things got a bit too fast for me! On the bike my ankle was fairly good but I had some difficulty in walking.

In the Milan Six, which started on the Monday, I was partnered with the Belgian, Emil Severeyns. He was a very good six day man and we had a great time together. It was a much easier Six with more rest than normal and plenty of diversions. These included dancing girls for the floor show in the track centre and, one way or another, we all had a very laughable week.

My ankle was much better by the end of the race but I picked up a very bad cold. The cabins below the track were terrifically hot. They were right next to the boiler house and the temperature never fell below 80°F. Sleeping for a few hours in that atmosphere and then going up to the colder stadium followed by sweating on the track all combined to make me chesty with a runny nose.

I wasn't very worried over it for I had had a few colds before and I went home to prepare for Paris–Nice. Before that I had a contract to ride the Antwerp Six but two days before the end I had to retire with 'flu. The cabins there were very hot but the place was full of draughts, especially at night, when all the Sportspaleis doors were open to let the people out.

As the weather was bitterly cold, I had a few days at home before going to Italy to ride the Genoa–Nice. I only did about fifty kilometres and then abandoned for I could not breathe properly and so, feeling very low, returned home once more.

I was too ill to ride Paris–Nice but had recovered somewhat by the time Milan–San Remo came up. But I soon found I was not fit, I had not got the strength in my legs, due to spending some time in bed, and lost any illusions about winning or even doing a good ride. I, therefore, retired at the bottom of the Poggio Hill, a few miles from the finish, as I did not see why I should continue and finish about 80th. I was still with the bunch but did not consider it worthwhile.

My next race was the five day Circuit du Provençal where I wanted to do a good ride. I had won the Tour of the South East some years back and this race had replaced it. We came to the last day and I was reasonably placed, although not one of the danger men. About two minutes down on general classification I attacked on the first climb and got away.

I was caught after a time by Anglade, Altig, and, you name them, they were all there! Another small break then got clear. I attacked again and went off in pursuit with

Frenchman Louis Rostollan. We caught the leaders and had soon whipped up a lead of about five minutes. The bunch chased very hard and as we reached a climb near Toulon, had got within one and a half minutes of us.

I hammered away on the climb and, over the top, when our lead had gone up to about six minutes. Most of the group were shattered now and were beginning to drop off. With about 30 miles to go, I found I was left with two other riders. Both were Belgians, Joseph Timmerman and Roger Baguet. Timmerman did his share of the work but Baguet, who was in Van Looy's team, would not do a stroke. They always claim to be protecting their leader or they have a man off the back. Anything to save them from working. Anything, in fact, to block the race.

On the road I was now the race leader, having some three minutes on the bunch. Towards Marseilles the mistral gave us hell, blowing us back along the rough, cobbled road. Our lead was slipping away with Baguet, still not doing a ha'p'orth of work, sitting on my wheel. As we came into the finish I thought, 'If he comes by me I'll push him into the bloody fence'. But, as it turned out, I just did not have the strength as he came by me with about 250 yards to the line. I could not even get out of the saddle I was so tired and finished behind both of them for third place on the stage and third place overall.

I then decided to ride the Tour of Belgium, more for training than anything else, but it was a disappointment. Before the start on the third day I was sitting in the team car and as I got out I knocked my instep on the bottom of the car door. I didn't take much notice of it at the time but on the following day it was very stiff and eventually I abandoned the ride in order to give it a rest and to prepare for Paris–Roubaix.

I rode quite well in this and got into the vital break. Un-

fortunately for me Van Looy was there with Sels and they
just controlled matters. I ended up sixth with my leg hurting quite a lot. The next day it was as stiff as hell so I went
to the doctor. He found that I had inflammation of a
tendon for which I had to have some injections. It also
meant I had to stay off the bike for a few days and I could
not train. Because of this I missed the Tour of Flanders. I
was not unfit, it was just that I knew I could not have won
it without training and I saw no point in riding just for the
sake of it.

Shortly afterwards I went to Germany and rode a race in
Dortmund, finishing seventh in terrible weather. Moving
on to Berlin I won the Grand Prix of Berlin behind the
motors and then returned for the Flèche Wallonne. This is
from Liége to Charleroi and it wasn't long before I was away
on my own. I was overtaken and, soon afterwards, the
Italian Poggiali broke away and I went after him taking
another Italian, Gimondi, with me.

I had not seen Gimondi before as he was a new professional. He would not work because he said his leader,
Adorni, was behind in the bunch. Poggiali, who was in a
different team, worked quite well and I flogged myself at
the front. B.F. that I am I did a lot of work thinking 'I can
beat these two nits'.

About three kilometres from the finish I attacked thinking that I could drop them but I was left behind instead
and finished third in a terrible state. I was glad though to
hear that Poggiali had won for I cannot stand riders who sit
in and never work and then take the pickings when everyone else is tired.

A few days later I was off on the Liége–Bastogne–Liége.
Coming out of Spa I attacked and the bunch split up. I
joined with a group at the front and attacked again, getting
clear with Gimondi. This time he worked a bit, perhaps

realising that he was better than he had thought. I dropped him after a few miles and then was caught myself. The weather was shocking with heavy rain and it was very cold.

I knew a descent a bit further on and I thought I would try there. It was a bad one with a bend, a level crossing and some very rough cobbles. The road sign said 'Slow' but I did the opposite and went at it fast. I took off into the air, made a perfect landing and was away up the road. I lost a bit of my lead on a big climb shortly afterwards but was still going well.

On the descent there was a very awkward bend. I was following a motor cyclist down, braking when he did. Into the corner and he got round with his big, fat tyres and I didn't! I hit the ground with an almighty bang, ripping lumps off my left arm. The bike was still all right and I remounted to be caught by the chasing group.

I stayed with them until the last climb coming into Liége where I was dropped. I was suffering now and my arm was giving me what for. Perhaps I was lucky, for there was another crash in the stadium where about six men came off on the wet track. Although I had passed a few of them when I came in I was placed eleventh as the organisers took my position from when I arrived on the track. They said the finish should not have been held there because it was too dangerous.

# 20

# Preparing for the Kill

I HEARD that Anquetil was entered for the Bordeaux–Paris race and so I decided to ride as well. I wanted to beat him and reckoned I could. Before that I had signed a contract to ride in England in the classic London–Holyhead race.

This, I knew, was a hard one, 275 miles non-stop and no pacing motors at all. It was only a week before the Bordeaux –Paris race but I thought I could manage it without any difficulty. After all I was very fit and only bad luck had stopped me from winning half a dozen times over the past few months.

I came over to London on the Friday night with Elliott, Denson, Hoban, the Belgian rider Van Meenan, Keith Butler and the Dane, Soni Kari. We had a laugh with Vin as we were coming up in the special coach from Southend Airport. While we were going along he suddenly said, 'By Gum! I'd like a pork pie and a pint of ale!' He kept asking the driver to stop and we kept telling him to keep going! Poor Vin! He never got his pie but I think he managed a pint when we got to our hotel.

It was there that another amusing incident took place. The start was at 5 a.m. from Marble Arch and breakfast at the hotel was timed for around three o'clock. The night porter called everyone easily as we all had 'phones in our rooms. I shall never forget him saying to me when I ans-

wered the phone, 'Good morning, sir. Time to get up for
your cycle rally!' Talk about laugh, I've never chuckled
so much before at that time in the morning! The description of the event as a 'rally' shows how knowledgeable
is the average member of the British public about bike
racing.

It was a grand race although the police were sometimes
unco-operative and some fans who tried to follow in cars
were often very stupid.

I shall always remember one motor cycle policeman. I
was in a small break with a few others, not far ahead of the
field, and we were approaching a set of traffic lights, something I have never had to think about in a bike race for
years! They were at red and Bill Bradley who was in the
break with me said, 'Don't go! Stay here, Tom, or he'll get
you!' I didn't understand him at all at first but did as I
was told and we stopped at the lights. When we moved off
on the green I saw what Bradley had meant. About 20
yards beyond the lights, hidden from us by a telephone box,
was a police motor cyclist. He even had the cheek to grin at
us when we went by!

Sometimes one was good and rode ahead of us waving
oncoming traffic over. I found this frightening, seeing heavy
lorries coming at you, for I was not used to racing on open
roads at all. Generally, however, for a race of this size, the
police co-operation was bad, but it fluctuated from county
to county.

The race followers were crazy. They cut in on us in the
bunch and drove in front of the race despite the officials
telling them to get away. They should have been ashamed of
themselves for they hindered the race, the officials and other
cars too. I was surprised to find how good some of the
British riders were and how bad were some of the others.
Eventually we had a good break going, eight of us together

for the last 50 or so miles. There were no more escapes and
we finished together. I won the sprint from Elliott with the
British Champion, Albert Hitchen, getting third place.

It was a record for the event, 10 hours 49 minutes and 4
seconds for the 275 miles. Almost motoring!

In spite of all the troubles I enjoyed it and found it a
great thrill to be riding again in my own country. I hope to
be able to come back and do it again sometime, but I think
the police ought to close the roads.

I returned home and prepared for Bordeaux–Paris. We
had quite a fast start which soon steadied itself. It was a
shocking night with rain pouring down and it was then, I
think, that I should have attacked Anquetil. He was tired
after his hectic 'plane journey to the start, for he had only
just finished another big race which he won.

Because it was so wet in the night we all made a gentleman's agreement to stop just before we picked up the
motors and change our wet clothes. We got off and began to
change in between the doors of the team cars. I wanted to
put a clean pair of shorts on and had put some grease in
them for it gives added protection in long races.

I took my shoes off to change my sodden socks, having a
clean vest and a jersey on, when suddenly I saw a Peugeot
rider go away. He had been riding behind the bunch for
most of the way changing his clothes as he went and now the
stupid nit attacked.

Everybody saw him go and a cry of 'The bastard' went up
and it was pandemonium! I struggled to get into my shoes
again, still wearing my wet, dirty socks, and I had considerable difficulty. The back of one shoe folded down and I had
no shoe horn so stood there at the roadside minus my shorts,
trying to get my shoe on. At last I succeeded and hurriedly
pulled on my clean pants, already greased.

Once these were on and the braces fixed I pulled another

jersey over my head and leapt on the bike. As I was belting off up the road I thought 'What on earth is this?' What had happened was that as I had put on my shorts, gravel from my socks and shoes had stuck in the grease and was now hurting like the devil!

So there I am, riding along digging my hands inside my shorts and pulling out lumps of gravel! I was still scraping gravel off my behind for some miles and was furious with Plaud. He had apparently made the arrangement for one of our riders to go away and had not told me. I was also very cross because the gentleman's agreement had been broken. I always believe in keeping an agreement like that whether it works out well for me or not and I was upset.

Plaud came alongside me in the team car and I told him to push off! He said he had arranged the attack to help me but, since he had not told me about it, I thought it was all a bit stupid. We soon picked up the motors and I then proceeded to have a most unfortunate ride. It seemed that every time an attack went my derny broke down. I had a spare pacemaker but it wasn't like having Ferdand Wambst in front.

Wambst must have broken down about six times in all. Things eventually sorted themselves out at the front and there was just Anquetil, Stablinski and myself away. Jacques had sat on my wheel for about 40-odd miles while Stablinski had been on his own in the lead and we were all together as we rode through the Valley of Chevreuse.

I was snookered now for they were team mates and so I was well and truly hammered. I was not going as well as I did in 1963 but, nonetheless, they had a hard job to get rid of me. I took quite a hiding as first Stablinski and then Anquetil attacked. I had to go everytime and they gradually wore me down. Some miles before the finish Anquetil went away and I could not hold him.

At the Parc des Princ I was still with 'Stab' but feeling
far from lively. As we came on to the track the sudden speed
cramped me up and he went ahead for second place, leaving me to take yet another third position. I was completely
down and had to be lifted off my bike. What did not help
was that Helen was there, she had never seen me win a race
and now, in my defeat and so close to me, she broke down
and cried. You can imagine the effect that had on me! It
was only a matter of seconds before I was at it too for I was
terribly disappointed.

Then, before the Tour de France, I had to ride in the
Midi Libre stage race. It was crazy really for I would
have been happy to take a rest and train for the Tour.
The Peugeot bosses said that I had to ride this four-day
race in order to earn my place in the Tour and so I had
little option.

On the last day of the race we had one of the younger
Peugeot riders, Roger Pingeon, in the leader's jersey. I was
content to protect him but watched Stablinski, for I had a
shrewd idea that he did not want a young man to win and
that he would have a go. He did and I got with the break
that he forced.

There was quite a group of us and we soon held a big
lead. I had ridden well earlier and so figured that I could
win. Coming towards the finish I felt very happy as I did
not even have to contest the sprint; all I had to do was finish
with the group to win. Round the final bend my back tyre
rolled off and down I went, only about a hundred yards
from the line too! I got a spare bike and rode in, but it was
too late and I was third.

I was terribly upset at this and thought the devil must be
working against me. Everything seemed to go wrong, no
matter how well I rode or how hard I tried. I knew when
things were right I was still the best but these mishaps and

disappointments were a very bitter pill. Just as in '61–62 I
was demoralised and unhappy.

About a week later I started the Tour de France feeling a
little better, both mentally and physically. I took things
steadily, for I reckoned I stood a fair chance of victory as
Anquetil was not riding this year. Unfortunately for me
about twenty other riders had the same idea and it was to
be a hard battle.

I started to come into my own in the mountains and on
the stage from Dax to Bagnères de Bigorre I pulled up from
36th to 7th place. This could perhaps have been better for I
crashed on the descent of the Aubisque. As I came down I
saw Van Looy a little way behind me. I wanted to catch the
leading group and certainly did not want to take the Belgian with me. Whatever the case, I went a bit too fast and it
was my own fault that I went over the edge. Luckily for me
it was a short drop and I only cut my hand, bruised my
elbows and tore my shorts and jersey. If I had gone over a
little further on I would have fallen several hundred feet
and that would have been the end of me!

I felt none the worse for wear and continued riding. Soon
we were on the flat again and heading for Barcelona. Again
I conserved my energy and waited for the Pyrenees. Before
that though we had the stage which finished at the top of
Mont Ventoux, the Giant of Provence. This is a great
mountain stuck out in the middle of nowhere and bleached
white by the sun. It is like another world up there among
the bare rocks and the glaring sun.

The white rocks reflect the heat and the dust rises clinging
to your arms, legs and face. I rode well up there doing about
five miles to the gallon in perspiration. It was almost over-
whelmingly hot up there and I think it was the only time that
I have got off my bike and my pants have nearly fallen
down. They were soaked and heavy with sweat which was

running off me in streams and I had to wring out my socks because the sweat was running into my shoes. We all must have lost pounds that day!

I was very content with the way things were going for I was now ninth overall, about seven minutes behind the leader Gimondi who was doing some great riding in his first Tour. After the next day's ride we arrived at Gap. I was feeling fine and had never felt better in the Tour. My hand hurt a little and a small abscess had come up but the Tour doctors had a look at it, performed a small operation cutting out the abscess and re-dressing the wound. I felt cheerful enough to telephone Helen that night and tell her I was going to pull out the stops over the next few days in the Pyrenees.

Later in the evening we moved our hotel because we could not sleep. It was past ten o'clock but next door some of the Tour drivers were having a film show and a bit of a 'do' with the locals and were making quite a row.

After a few hours' sleep we started off on our ride to Briançon but as we reached the first big climb, the Col de Vars, I found I could not breathe properly. I creaked and groaned my way up. Everybody passed me, even Belgian Beheyt, and I nearly fell off in surprise!

On the flat I recovered a little and made up some lost ground, but when we reached the lower slopes of the Izoard climb I went backwards again. I felt dreadful now and the doctor came alongside to give me something to help my breathing. It was no use. Everyone went by me and our mechanic put a tiny gear on a back wheel for me in the car. He came out later and changed the wheel but that did not help either. I was just crawling along and felt very ill.

Vin Denson came alongside and said: 'Do you want a drink of lemonade, Tom?' 'No,' said I. 'Would you like some fresh water then, I've just got some from a spring?'

'No!' I said, more sharply. 'Shall I give you a push?' he said. Dear old big-hearted Vin was so surprised when I replied 'No, push off and leave me alone!' I had not meant to hurt his feelings but I just wanted to be left on my own, to suffer without anyone else there. Rather like an elephant going away to die.

At Briançon it was found that I had bronchitis and I could only think that I picked it up when we moved hotels in the night at Gap. It was very cold that night and it must have affected me. The curious thing was that I had put on weight that day and could not understand it. I slept well but next morning could not open my eyes. My face was all puffed and I had to dip it in cold water to get my eyes open properly.

I went down to the start feeling like death warmed up and as we reached the first climb, off I went. My hand was swelling up again and another abscess was showing in the palm, making it difficult to hold the handlebars because of the pain. My inability to grip made the climbs more hard, but I slogged on though losing time all the way.

At Aix-les-Bains I finished just inside the time limit, completely exhausted. I had beaten the elimination and all I aimed to do now was hang on until we reached Paris. That night I was examined thoroughly by the doctors who made tests on my blood and water. They found out that I had an infection of the kidneys, just to make matters worse! They also operated again on my hand but it seemed to make little difference.

Anyhow, I started again the next day on the time trial stage up Mont Revard. I finished last but I was still there. All hopes of doing anything notable had long since departed and, as on my first Tour, all I wanted to do was reach the end.

It had become normal now for me to douse my face in

water to get my eyes open and the following morning I could
still just hang on. I struggled along to Lyons and ended the
day in last place, about 15 minutes down. I didn't care any
more about anything for I was just about on my knees.

The stage to Auxerre was my lot. Some five miles from
the start I was off for I just could not find any more strength.
My whole body ached. Even my right hand was aching because I had been gripping tighter on the 'bars with it as my
other hand was useless. Every little bump on the road jarred
me and I had to give in.

I was almost sobbing with pain and disappointment when
they put me into the ambulance and took me to the hospital
at Auxerre. The doctor there was appalled at my condition
and said that unless I had an immediate operation on my
hand, I was in danger of losing it but as I had eaten something for breakfast before the stage began, they would not
operate. Instead, they filled me up with penicillin and arranged for me to be taken to Paris by helicopter the next
morning. I had insisted on this as Helen would be waiting
for me in Paris and she would not want to come all the way
out to Auxerre. The next morning I was whisked away and
operated on that night. They left me quiet for a while and
filled me with more penicillin to deal with the blood poisoning. I also had to have a couple of 'drainpipes' put in my
hand for a time. After five days I returned home, absolutely
dead beat and very miserable. The Tour had got me again.

# 21

# Moment of Triumph

IT WAS not a good omen for the winning of the world title. For ten days I stayed at home, taking it easy and not even touching my bike. Gradually I began to feel my strength returning and mentally I felt much better too. I realised that I had been unfortunate, but like the old story of Bruce and the spider, I had to try again and I settled down to a training programme. I worked this out for myself as I had no contracts to keep except a ride at the Crystal Palace again at the end of July. It was good to return to England but it was a harder race there than previously and finished with Michael Wright the winner. I was sixth in the sprint and had to be content with my showing over the 50 miles. I did another couple of contract rides and then slipped into oblivion for a bit, concentrating on my training.

I took it steadily at first, doing about 25 miles only for a few days. Then, day by day, I rode further. Thirty, then forty and forty-five miles and I could feel my form surging back. I got that old, confident feeling again and I was a happy man once more.

When I reached the point where I could do seventy miles, fast, I managed to get a contract to ride a criterium event at Mende. I thought that I would really try here and see what I could do under pressure. Things went very well and I was quite pleased with the result, for I finished third after six riders had got away and taken a lap on the field. In spite of this I jumped away and caught them, so I felt good at having taken the lap on my own and was more than satisfied with my progress.

The next I entered was the Paris–Luxembourg stage race, but I had no intention of doing any good rides and used each stage for training purposes. It worked to my advantage in more ways than one for, by keeping out of the picture, I was still an 'unfavourite' for the world title.

On the first day I rode quietly in the bunch and when we started the second stage felt in good form. Still unwilling to show myself at the front I worked from the back, bringing up some of our team who had had trouble. The first one was George Van Conningsloo, who punctured. I stopped and waited for him, pacing him back up to the bunch. We were hardly back before Ramsbottom crashed on some tram lines in Charleroi and, once more, I waited. I got him back on and, I think, in all that day I went back and forth about seven times. I 'blew up' on a climb just before the stage finish and lost about fourteen minutes, but it did not worry me much.

The important thing to me was that I had made a number of strenuous efforts during the stage and had felt all right. I did the majority of the work in getting the others back on to the field and had punished myself quite severely without too much effect. On the last day I again made myself do a lot of work, although I never featured in any of the key moves but found enough to do in closing gaps and generally forcing myself to ride hard for no immediate reward.

I came home feeling fine and brimful of confidence and now talked myself into winning the worlds. I drummed it into my head that I was going to win and nothing and nobody could stop me. Only bad luck would make me fail and I reckoned that, after all this time, I was due for a break.

The championships were being held in Lasarte, near San Sebastian in Spain, and I drove down there with plenty of time to spare, sharing the driving with the Australian Nev Veale. I had not brought a *soigneur* this time for I thought I would look after myself. If anything went wrong then I could only blame myself for it and not any doctors or team managers.

I arrived in San Sebastian a few days before the event and took things quietly at my hotel, but did a little training round the circuit. This was quite hilly and its total distance was about eleven and three-quarter miles, with fourteen laps to be covered.

As often happens it started to rain and it was still pouring when the great day came round. Everyone knows the phrase about the rain in Spain, but this was beyond imagination. I had thought, on looking at the circuit earlier, that it was not difficult enough for a championship, but now the rain was streaming down it was a different matter.

There were ninety-six riders when the long grind began, which was to last some six and a half hours. As we were coming through to begin the second lap I heard someone in the crowd shout something about a minute up. As the British riders had agreed to help me if they could I looked round for Rams, found him and asked him if there was a break. 'Yes,' he said. 'There's about a dozen of them up there. Barry's with them and Post and Swerts?' 'Bloody hell!' I said. 'Give me a hand to get up, will you?' Whereupon he and Vin Denson took me to the front of the bunch and led me out. As I went off the front there was a bit of a dash by a few other riders, but I put my head down, kept going and, in about fifty yards, swung over. Altig came through with a Spaniard on his wheel but there was no-one behind them. We raced away, working well together, and caught the break by the time the third lap began.

All the Spaniards there, five of them, were going well at the front and so was Post and Den Hartog, the two Dutchmen. Also with us were two Italians, Meali and Balmanion, another German, Kunde, the Belgian Roger Swerts who was doing no work at all, myself and Hoban and the Swiss rider, Bingelli.

We set about keeping clear and soon were nearly three minutes up on the bunch. Just about the halfway mark we got news that another break had detached itself from the main field and were chasing at about two and a half minutes. In it was the Belgian Sels and Stablinski. We certainly did not want that little lot with us and so pushed along a bit harder.

Swerts was still not doing a stroke and neither were the Italians, Den Hartog or the Swiss. Post, Altig, the Spanish riders and I were all going like the clappers at the front, and Barry? He almost flogged his eyeballs out! We kept away from them and were glad to hear that they were back in the bunch. I began to be vexed about the non-workers for I reckoned we would tow them all the way and then they would just come up for the sprint, something I did not want. I really only feared two men there, Altig and Post. Altig was probably on good form although he was on crutches when the Tour de France started.

I wondered if he had the necessary miles in his legs and considered Post to be the more dangerous. As we came through the finishing straight to complete ten laps I was wondering if and when I should attack. One of the Spaniards had come off with a puncture, but otherwise we were all together.

I hung on a bit longer. I did not want to go on my own for I was a bit worried then about keeping away over that distance. So, I bided my time. I was definitely going to attack and try to break this group up, for there were still some dangerous sprinters there including some who had done no work and were full of fight.

About halfway round the circuit and coming up for just two laps to the finish, I went ahead. It was timed to a nicety as I attacked on the big climb near the village of Hernani. I was using my championship ring on the back wheel, the 54 × 14, and I kept it in as we went up the climb. In a matter of yards I was clear, taking Altig with me. I was a bit surprised that no one else came up but was quite satisfied to have the German there. He was a good worker and as we reached the top of the hill, I said to him, 'Come on, Rudi, remember the Barrachi!' We had been partners in the Barrachi Trophy event last year and he had shattered me. I was so dead he had practically pushed me over the last few miles.

I think that must have made him think he could win. He just smiled and nodded and we got down to the work of keeping clear. As we began the thirteenth lap we had a lead of about a minute. Behind, the group had split with Post, Den Hartog and Swerts coming after us leaving the others straggling along.

I was keen to get on with the job now and confident of victory. I knew that I could beat Altig and it was now merely a question of keeping the others at bay. On we went, taking our turn at the front. I think Altig did his share although I was trying hard enough too. He was going through very fast as I moved across after my stint and, each time he did this, I had to push a bit to hold him.

Eventually I told him not to go through so fast and I think he figured that I was a bit shattered. Soon it was his turn to complain, for just as we went over the Hernani climb he asked me not to attack on the hills. I was a better climber and, no doubt, was pushing a bit hard up the climbs. He did not realise it but he signed his own death warrant when he said that for I knew then that I could beat him. Although he was a dangerous man in a sprint I knew, somehow or other, that I could get past him.

Up to then I had thought about breaking away on the hills but now I was not bothered. What, in fact, had worried me was that if I did break way alone I might 'blow up' as I had done on many occasions before. That had been my one fear, apart from Swerts coming through, for I think I would have cried had he won. I hate riders who don't work and then just come through to take the glory. I don't mind anybody beating me if he's done his share but I cannot abide the 'wheel-suckers', as I have said before.

Soon we were on the last lap, the final eleven and three-quarter miles, and I was confident I was going to win. I cannot explain it, call it intuition or what you like, but I could not accept the fact that Altig could beat me. Going round the back of the circuit we came to a gentleman's agreement. Both of us had worked hard in our little break and, therefore, we each deserved an equal chance of victory. We agreed to separate when we reached the 'one kilometre' to go board and ride in side by side. In this way there would be no tactical advantage for either of us and it would be a straight sprint for the line. Altig was quite happy about this for I am sure he thought he could put it across me.

So, there we were, two gentlemen virtually fighting a duel over the last kilometre. I was glad that Altig had accepted my proposal for it was the fairest way out. I have always regarded him as a great rider and his showing that day did nothing to make me change my mind.

I led all the way down that final descent and through the packed, cheering streets of Lasarte. As we approached the kilometre sign we dutifully parted and came towards the line side by side. I started my sprint a few hundred yards out and kept going as hard as I could. I didn't look ahead at all, I was looking down, looking for his shadow on the road as he came up on me. I kept thinking, 'He's coming! He's coming! He's coming!' And, suddenly when I was ten yards from the line it dawned on me. 'He hasn't! He hasn't made it! It's Mine!' and I was over the line, grinning like a maniac, heart pounding and tears welling up in my eyes.

Dear Albert Beurick, my staunch Belgian friend, wearing a Great Britain racing cap of all things, got to me first. I have never seen his twenty stone move so fast, and, crying like a child, he lifted me, bike and all, right off the road. I was champion of the world at last!

It took some little time for it to sink in. Not even on the rostrum did it seem real, in spite of the congratulations, cheers and back-slapping. It might somehow have been somebody else who had won. It was not until I was back at the hotel and had a quick glass of champagne with the other members of the British team that it began to dawn on me that I had achieved what I set out to do nearly fifteen years earlier. These men were my friends and being cyclists themselves knew what it meant. Praise from them was really something.

Gaston Plaud, my Directeur Sportif, was there and I remembered how, as I finished, I caught sight of him with tears of joy running down his face and I remember too how it was Ramsbottom who gave me the first clue that I had at last succeeded. He is not an emotional type but just a good, solid Lancashire lad and his reaction shook me. I had just finished the race and was waiting at the roadside for the rest of the field to come in. As Alan crossed the line he just let his bike fall to the ground and ran towards me arms outstretched and his glasses streaked with tears. As he reached me he threw his arms round me and kissed me on both cheeks in true continental fashion! It was incidents like this which helped me realise that at last I had succeeded.

Almost immediately after the quick glass of champagne I had to leave for Biarritz to catch a 'plane to go to Paris where I was contracted for another ride. On the way I became lost in thought to such an extent that when we boarded the 'plane I left behind my bag with my gold medal and champion's jersey. As a result I had to borrow some shorts from Poulidor, shoes and socks from Stablinski and a world champion's jersey from Jan Janssen the next day in Paris. Incidentally, Jean Stablinski, who had shared a room with me when we arrived in Paris, was very generous with his praise : 'It does me good to see you as a world champion. I have never seen anyone so pleased before. I woke up last night about three times and there you were, lying in your bed with a big grin on your face. You were fast asleep because I spoke to you and you did not answer.'

I cannot know how true this is, but I do know that for a little while I could understand how Cassius Clay must have felt when he won the world boxing championship. I was on top of the world and was happy for everyone.

One effect however was that my riding went completely to pieces and for the next few days I was terrible.

It may be that I was shaken, that first day in Paris when I looked at my bike for the first time since it was swept away from under me in a pandemonium of cheering and back slapping immediately after winning the championship. As I looked at the tyres I found that the rear one had a two inch strip worn away, with strands of rubber hanging free, it was bulging at the side and was on the point of bursting at any moment. I have no idea how long it had been like this, but obviously fate had been on my side that wet September day in Spain.

My thoughts are now with the future, which seems bright. I am no longer eternally second, the man who so nearly but not quite won everything. There is no doubt that the title affected my racing, giving me more confidence, for in October of the same year I won the Tour of Lombardy. Oddly enough, I was away with Motta again, just as in 1964, but this time I had a rainbow jersey on my back and I left the Italian in the last six miles to win alone. The Press acclaimed this as my greatest ever victory, even better than the world championship. I hope there are many more to come.

Most of all I would like to win the Tour de France, but I cannot afford to have any bad luck, such as in past attempts. If I fail it will not have been for the want of trying!

As I look back now all the sacrifices, aches and disappointments seem worth it, although I sometimes wonder if I could go through it again. Disappointments are always hard to bear at the time but common sense tells you that there is always another day tomorrow for you have to have another go. There are always more milestones ahead, no matter how many you have passed. The only thing I fear is when I am too old to ride. There is nothing else I have wanted to be other than a good racing cyclist. So far I have enough money for the immediate needs of my family and, even more important, I have made a lot of friends.

Since I started on this book I have broken a leg, having had a couple of skiing accidents on exactly the same day in successive years. This makes me wonder if bad luck is dogging me still but I am not moaning. I remember hearing somewhere that people who succeed may do so with luck but generally it is spelled 'pluck' with the 'p' silent.

But there is one thing in which I have had all the luck in the world and nothing can ever take away what it has meant to me. I mean that apart from countless friends, advisers and well-wishers there are three people in my life to whom I owe more than I can say. They are my father, my mother and Helen, my wife. Each has put up with a great deal and if I have never said much to them about being grateful, I'm saying it now. I hope there are many more milestones which together we shall reach.